Redeemer Lutheran Church
61 Mississippi Way NE
Fridley, MN 55432
Phone: (763)574-7445
Fax: (763)574-2081

July 2006

Dear Pastor:

I am pleased to send you UNDERSTANDING HOMOSEXUALITY:
PERSPECTIVES FOR THE LOCAL CHURCH. This complimentary copy
comes to you as a leader in this church through the generosity of a sister ELCA
congregation in Colorado. Their conviction is that the message of this book
needs to get out.

In recent years, homosexuality has more and more moved unto center stage in
the local, synodical, and Churchwide arenas. The 2005 Churchwide Assembly
acted on resolutions dealing with the blessing of same-sex unions and the
ordination of practicing same-sex church leaders. The ELCA is currently in the
midst of developing a social policy statement on human sexuality that is
scheduled to be brought before the 2009 Churchwide Assembly for action. It is
more important than ever, then, that we do not simply ignore the issue as
inconsequential or unimportant. Indeed, it has become impossible to ignore.
It is more important than ever to be able to intelligently discuss and rationally
respond to the two main questions people in our churches are asking: "Is
homosexual behavior contrary to the will of God?" and "What should be the
church's attitude toward same-sex persons?" UNDERSTANDING
HOMOSEXUALITY is a book that addresses these critical questions.

Dr. Robert Benne, in his back cover endorsement, states that the book's
comprehensiveness will be a help in sorting out and assessing our churchly
debates surrounding homosexuality. Dr. Merton Strommen commends the
book as an excellent reference for use in a congregation. To that end, please
accept this book as a gift to you. This edition includes a Study Guide that
might be helpful in using the book in a Bible Study or small group
environment.

The two Sunday morning messages on the CD - "Hope for the Homosexual"
and "The Truth about Homosexuality" - is one attempt to address this
emotional and sensitive issue in a congregational setting.

Sincerely,


Dr. David N. Glesne

Should you desire to make this book available for group study, Kirk House Publishers will arrange for quantity discount for congregations or organizations.

> 5 to 10 books      15%
> 11 to 20 books    20%
> 21 or more books 30%

Please contact the publisher at:
> publisher@kirkhouse.com
> 1-888-696-1828
> Fax: 952-835-1828

> Kirk House Publishers
> PO Box 390759
> Minneapolis, MN 55439

You may order from the online catalog at

www.kirkhouse.com

# *Study Guide*

## Introduction

1.  Do you agree or disagree that the identified issues in the introduction are crucial questions facing the church today? Discuss and respond to these questions.

2.  Discuss the story told by Richard Hays of Gary thinking through before God the relation between his homosexuality and his Christian faith. What part do ideological voices play in the current discussion of homosexuality in society and in the church?

## Chapter One:  Four Common Myths

1.  As your discussion begins, how would you personally answer the two major questions facing the church with regard to homosexuality? What could cause you to alter your response?

2.  In what ways can cultivating friendships with self-identified homosexual persons benefit a person in thinking through this matter of homosexuality?

3.  Discuss the four common myths presented in this chapter. Are they real or not? In what ways do they affect the current debate?

4.  The chapter ends by saying that every one of us is battling something in our lives and that we are not as different from one another as we may think. In what way can this reality change our attitudes toward homosexual persons?

## Chapter Two: Causes of Homosexuality

1.  If, according to the American Psychiatric Association's Office on International Affairs (1993), a majority of psychiatrists internationally view homosexuality as a developmental disorder, how does this fact affect your understanding of the homosexual condition?

2.  Discuss Jeffrey Satinover's quote on p. 39 in light of the considerable evidence pointing to early family relationships, early homosexual experiences, and genetic predisposition as contributing factors in becoming homosexual. How would you answer someone who asks, "What causes homosexuality?"

3. Lesbian philosopher and activist Camille Paglia says, "No one is born gay. The idea is ridiculous…homosexuality is an adaptation, not an inborn trait." What is the difference between the "born gay" theory and substantial evidence for the influence of genetic predisposition in some homosexual persons?

4. What is the basis of morality? Does genetic and biological research affect the morality of a situation? Can morality be decided on the basis of genes?

## Chapter Three: The Gay Lifestyle and Agenda

1. Would you consider Dr. Monteith's research findings concerning the kinds and frequencies of behavior engaged in by homosexual persons to be normal? healthy and life-giving?

2. Research by Paul Cameron (<u>Does Homosexual Behavior Shorten Lifespan?</u>) reveals that the average lifespan of a promiscuous homosexual person is nearly 40% shorter than the average American male. Those homosexual persons *with* long-term partners fare even worse. Why do you think those in monogamous, committed relationships fare even worse?

3. Evaluate how effectively the strategic homosexual agenda for America put forth in Kirk and Madsen's <u>After the Ball</u> (1989) has been implemented since then.

## Chapter Four: Four Christian Views

1. Do you think homosexual behavior is seen by many today as the "worst of sins?" What would you say to one who believes this?

2. How do you respond to the lesser of two evil's argument? to the Bible not being relevant to our contemporary social situation argument?

3. The interpretive context for the third view is a particular cultural and religious setting. The interpretive context for the fourth view is the creation accounts in Genesis. How do these different interpretive settings produce different views of the Bible's relevance for today?

## Chapter Five: The Great Divide-Biblical Authority

1. This chapter claims that on one side of the homosexual debate the authority of the Bible comes essentially from man's initiative and on the

other side, from God's initiative. Should the human interpretation of the text be the final authoritative word or should God's revelation in the text be the final authoritative word?

2.    Discuss the relationships between God, Scripture, and faith in the story of the telephone call about the house burning. Can one believe in Christ (the messenger) without believing the Scriptures (the message about Christ)?

3.    When you read your Bible, how do you understand what you are reading? Are they human words in which people are attempting to understand God's ways? Are they human words through which God is speaking His Word to you?

## Chapter Six: Interpreting the Bible

1.    What is meant by saying that while we take the Bible in its literal sense, not everything in the Bible is to be read literalistically?

2.    What might be better words to use today instead of the words "literal" and "interpretation?"

3.    In what way are we to read the Bible like we read the morning newspaper?

4.    In order to come to greater understanding of the Bible, what are some steps we can take to "bridge the gap" between ourselves and the people to whom the Bible was given?

5.    In order to come to greater understanding of the Bible, we need to "remove our glasses" and set aside preconceived notions and ideas. Are you aware of any of these in yourself? in others? Why is it so difficult to remove our glasses?

## Chapter Seven: The Heterosexual Norm

1.    The author believes the place to begin the discussion regarding homosexuality is not with the few places in Scripture where homosexual acts are mentioned, but with the Genesis creation accounts. Why does he believe this? Do you agree or disagree? Why?

2.    Was Jesus "silent" about homosexuality or does Jesus' teaching on marriage in Matthew 19 speak to same-sex intercourse inasmuch as his perspective on marriage speaks loud and clear?

3. In what way does God's creation of the complimentarity of the male and female body and their structures speak of God's intention for human sexuality?

4. Discuss the four things that can be learned about the nature of the marriage union from the Genesis creation accounts. In what way does heterosexual marriage in Genesis speak into the homosexual debate today?

## Chapter Eight:  Old Testament Biblical Fences Around Marriage

1. Retell the stories of the men of Sodom (Genesis 19:1-11) and the Levite and his concubine (Judges 19:22-25). What has been the traditional understanding of the homosexual behavior in these stories? What are the new arguments? Evaluate the old and the new arguments.

2. Read Leviticus 18:22 and 20:13. What is the traditional understanding? What are the new arguments being put forth today? Evaluate each.

3. What are the three major classes or kinds of Old Testament laws? Why do the ceremonial and civil laws no longer apply to the Christian? Why are Christians to continue to obey the moral law?

## Chapter Nine:  New Testament Fences Around Marriage

1. In Romans 1:26-27 do you think Paul is talking about homosexual persons committing homosexual acts or heterosexual persons committing homosexual acts? Give reasons.

2. The author states that along with the creation accounts, Romans 1 is the clearest passage in the Scriptures which answers the question of the moral rightness or wrongness of homosexual behavior. Why would you agree or disagree?

3. Read I Corinthians 6:9-11. Why do so many find such great hope for same-sex persons in these verses?

4. Read I Timothy 1:9-10. Which of the 10 Commandments does "sodomites" appear to be connected with? What importance might this moral context have in the current debate?

5. How would you answer the question, "Is homosexual behavior contrary to the will of God?"

## Chapter Ten: Analogy Arguments

1. Gentile Inclusion Analogy: Discuss the alleged category confusions and dissimilarities between the issue of Gentile inclusion (Acts 15) and homosexuality. Is the analogy a convincing one? Why or why not?

2. Slavery Analogy Argument: Discuss the claim that nowhere does Scripture command or encourage or sanction slavery. Rather, the Scriptures regulate existing situations. Is the slavery analogy argument a good one? Why or why not?

3. Divorce/Remarriage Analogy: Do you think the church has been faithful or unfaithful in upholding the teaching of Jesus and Scripture on divorce and remarriage? Why? Is the analogy a good one in arguing for acceptance of homosexuality? Why or why not?

4. Women in Ministry: Do you think that the argument put forward that as the Church changed its view and practice of women in ministry, so it should also change its view and accept committed homosexual unions in the Church is a convincing one? Why or why not?

## Chapter Eleven: Attitudes and Understanding

1. Discuss this chapter's call for the Church to repent of its attitudes of rejection and scorn of homosexual persons. Do you agree or disagree that repentance is the place to start? Discuss the need for a "double repentance."

2. Humility: Why is there no ground for self-righteous condemnation of homosexual behavior?

3. Love: Have you ever seen a lack of love expressed for homosexual persons? Share with others. Have you ever seen love expressed for homosexual persons but that love rejected as unloving? Share.

4. Acceptance: Discuss Jesus' acceptance of the woman of Samaria while not approving of her behavior. What is involved in accepting my homosexual neighbor while at the same time not approving of his/her behavior?

5. Compassion: Compassion is not only having pity for but doing something to meet human need. How can we show compassion for same-sex persons?

# Chapter Twelve:  Communities of Grace

1.	What can a local church do to educate its members on current issues of human sexuality?  What can your church do?

2.	What can a local church do to become a safe place for strugglers of all stripes to find grace and love and the power of release from the self-destructive grip of addictions and compulsions?

3.	How are love and law related to one another in the Scriptures?  Can one person do an unloving thing towards another in the name of love?  Share instances.

4.	Before God, do we have the right to define for ourselves what we can do on the basis of desires that we experience in life, or does God have the right to transform us into the image of Jesus as God sees fit?  Discuss this matter of rights.

5.	How would you answer the question, "What is to be the Church's attitude toward homosexual persons?"

# Chapter Thirteen:  Communities of Truth

1.	Why is discipline in the church such a difficult concept?  On those rare but necessary occasions when the church is called to discipline one of its own, what is to be the motive and purpose of the discipline?

2.	Should the church bless same-sex unions?  Why or why not?

3.	Should practicing same-sex persons be ordained?  Why or why not?

4.	Discuss the calling of the church to walk the tight rope of holding on to truth and speaking this truth in love.  How can we do this?

# Understanding Homosexuality

Perspectives for the Local Church

by David N. Glesne

Kirk House Publishers
Minneapolis, Minnesota

# Understanding Homosexuality
## Perspectives for the Local Church

by David N. Glesne

Copyright 2004 David N. Glesne.  All rights reserved

Library of Congress Cataloging-inPublication data

Understanding homosexuality : perspectives for the local church / by David N. Glesne.

     p.cm.

  Includes bibliographic references

  ISBN-10: 1-886513-95-5 (perfect bound : alk. paper)
  ISBN-13: 978-1-886513-95-2

    1. Homosexuality—religious aspects. 2. Gays—religious life. I. Title.

BL65.H64G54 2005
261.8'35766—dc22

                        20055043213

Kirk House Publishers, PO Box 390759, Minneapolis, MN 55439
Manufactured in the United States of America

# Table of Contents

# Prologue

Ronald sat down next to me for the Monday evening meal. He had just arrived at St. Deiniol's, a residential library in northeastern Wales, from Manchester, England, having just attended *Half Way to Lambeth*, the annual conference of the Lesbian and Gay Christian Movement. We immediately struck up a lively conversation.

Ronald was working on a PhD in what he considers homophobic translations of three Old Testament passages. I was spending eight weeks at the library writing on a pastoral response to gay and lesbian people. We quickly got into rich conversation over the biblical passages – the meaning of Hebrew words and matters of interpretation.

I learned that Ronald, now in his late 50s, has been openly gay since age 24. He grew up in a Danish Lutheran church but now is in the Quaker church. As I listened closely, I could hear the pain of rejection and the deep hurt that church people had caused him. I sensed the loneliness and alienation he had felt in past years. I saw the anger that swelled up from within as he spoke of homophobia in the church. Here was a deeply wounded man sitting next to me.

I was moved as I listened to his experiences with the Church. "How could God's people have been so insensitive?" I thought. "Why could they not have befriended him rather than turned a cold shoulder? What could I do?" I am a pastor in the Body of Christ and here was one wounded deeply by the Church's lack of love. I perhaps couldn't do much but I could do something.

I turned to Ronald and said, "Ronald, will you forgive us? I am a part of the Church of Jesus Christ and we as a Church have sinned against you and God by the way we have wronged you. We have not loved you as we ought. I am ashamed of the way some of us in the Body have treated you. Our attitudes and actions have been very wrong and displeasing to God. I repent of the part I have played and want to forgo any pride or prejudice or homophobia there may be in me. We are sorry and ask you to forgive us."

Ronald sat motionless for a few moments. Finally he broke the silence. "I'm not sure I can get up and throw my arms around you right now," he said. But he thanked me. We continued talking but after a few minutes he returned to a thought. He told me that he would be speaking to a gay and lesbian group the coming Saturday and that he had been planning to tell them that he thought the Christian Church was 500 years away from confessing to gays and lesbians how much it had wronged them. He then paused and said, "I'll maybe have to change what I was going to say to them."

Could this be the place to start? In the past, society has rejected homosexual persons and then when they have come to our churches they have felt the same rejection causing many to start churches and organizations of their own. Maybe the way forward through this tangled sexual mess is the Church repenting and asking gays and lesbians for forgiveness for the way we have treated them. Such authenticity may be the only thing that will arrest the attention of those who have not experienced the love and compassion of Jesus Christ in and through the Church. Maybe a change of the Church's mind and heart is essential to a prescription for a healthy church life in which Christian homophiles can be fully welcomed members.

# Introduction

At the time of this writing, the Evangelical Lutheran Church in America is undertaking an extensive study on the question whether or not to bless same-sex unions and ordain persons in committed same-sex relationships. Other larger denominations of the Christian church have undertaken similar studies in recent years. For many in the churches, these ongoing studies have become an exasperation since the Scriptures and the moral tradition of the church seem to speak to the issue with unambiguous clarity. For others, an equal frustration and impatience has grown because they feel it is taking the church so long to recognize homosexual persons as fully participating members of the church.

What is clear, however, is that the laity and leaders of the church must face the issue and deal with it. Those who are exasperated and frustrated may tend to look at this present time as a time of great peril for the church. However, it may be not only a necessary time of examination, but a time of advantage. As unsettling as the homosexual issue is, the study of it may bring to light side issues that would not otherwise be seen by the laity of the church.

Just as with indulgences in the time of Luther, homosexuality touches the nerve of many critical theological and spiritual questions. It grips the attention of lay people and threatens the financial base of church wide ministries. It is therefore possible that renewal and reformation of many aspects of the church's thought and life can emerge from the necessary reflection needed on this issue. Approval of the blessing of same-sex unions and the ordination of avowed and practicing homosexual persons would be a logical outcome of recent developments in the church's theology, biblical understanding and sexual mores which have had little close scrutiny among the mass of the laity. The homosexual issue dramatizes the direction of certain trends in theology today and brings the end result into the light for all to see. As a result the church is being forced to face some crucial questions:

Is the Reformation conviction of *Sola Scriptura* still supreme for the church's faith and life? What role does church tradition, human reason, and human experience play in moral and ethical guidance? What is the church to do when new interpretations of biblical passages contradict the long-standing understanding of the church's teaching?

Are people accepted and approved by God because of the grace and love of Jesus Christ regardless of their attitudes toward Him and their behavior with others? Or is a person called to repentance and faith in Christ which brings forgiveness of sins and issues forth in growth in holiness of life?

Is the situation ethic of love alone as the criterion by which to judge every human relationship an adequate moral guide today? Should the church approve of all sexual activity that is loving in nature even though this activity takes place outside the bounds of the traditional limits of gender, marriage and the family?

Should the church approve of alternate life styles in its sexual morality? Or is there a core biblical sexual ethic that negates such alternative life styles?

If the laity and leaders of the church ask these questions seriously, a biblical and theological awakening could renew the church in our day.

The name of this book is reflective of the context out of which it is written. While theologians and biblical scholars have generated an enormous literature on the subject of the Bible and homosexuality, I write as the pastor of a local church. The book is born out of the experiences of one ministering on a daily basis in a congregational setting to the joys and sorrows of people struggling with a variety of life issues – including homosexual experiences. It is also born out of a deep sense of call to clarify to the best of one's ability the Scripture's teachings on the breadth of issues confronting people today.

By virtue of theological training I have one foot in the world of academia and, by calling, the other foot in the arena of pastoral ministry. Having said that, I make no pretense to be a biblical scholar. I write from the perspective of a pastor who teaches and preaches and counsels in a local church setting. The contents of this writing, therefore, have come from biblical studies taught, sermons preached, and discussions engaged in with lay people in the local church.

There are three groups of people in mind in this writing. First, the non-specialist but thinking Christian in the pew who is saying, "I'm confused. I need to think this issue through. My heart is telling me one thing. My head is telling me another." This confusion has come for many in getting to know relatives or friends or fellow church members who are gay or lesbian and who seem like wonderful people and good Christians, and they do not understand how that can be. People are confused and want to know what the Bible says about two main questions: "Is homosexuality contrary to the will of God?" and "What should be the church's attitude toward the homosexual?" People are confused because they thought they knew what the Bible says about homosexuality, but are now being told that understanding may not be correct. They are sincerely looking to the church for help in figuring out what God thinks about all this.

The second group that is in mind is those men and women, young and old, who are experiencing deep suffering as a result of homosexual desires and feelings they wish they did not have. There are Christians and non-Christians both inside and outside the church who feel alienated from all camps on the current homosexuality landscape. They tend to make these camps feel uncomfortable and so feel isolated from them. They often have no one in whom they can safely confide. Some of these have grown up in environments in which the subject of homosexuality was taboo, or worse, environments riddled with gay bashing and cruel jokes. At the same time, these people do not feel represented by the gay rights movement. They cannot celebrate their homosexual desires and feelings or fully embrace the homosexual lifestyle because they are convinced, for a variety of reasons, that their homoerotic desires are the result of something having gone terribly wrong. Many of these people long for freedom from what they experience as an unhealthy compulsion and seek help to change.

Richard Hays, Professor of New Testament at Duke Divinity School, tells of such a person. He writes about his best friend from college, Gary, who came to spend a week with his family shortly before dying of AIDS. They spent much time talking and reminiscing about everything from politics to the Vietnam War to the Beatles. But Gary had come not only to say good-bye but once again to think through before God the relation between his homosexuality and his Christian faith. Hays writes:

"[Gary] was angry at the self-affirming gay Christian groups, because he regarded his own condition as more complex and tragic than their apologetic stance could acknowledge. He also worried that the gay subculture encouraged homosexual believers to 'draw their identity from their sexuality' and thus to shift the ground of their identity subtly and idolatrously away from God. For more than twenty years, Gary had grappled with his homosexuality, experiencing it as a compulsion and an affliction. Now as he faced death, he wanted to talk it all through again from the beginning, because he knew my love for him and trusted me to speak without dissembling....

In particular, Gary wanted to discuss the biblical passages that deal with homosexual acts....He had read hopefully through the standard bibliography of the burgeoning movement advocating the acceptance of homosexuality in the church....In the end, he came away disappointed, believing that these authors, despite their good intentions, had imposed a wishful interpretation on the biblical passages. However much he wanted to believe that the Bible did not condemn homosexuality, he would not violate his own stubborn intellectual integrity by pretending to find their arguments persuasive....Gary, as a homosexual Christian, believed that their writings did justice neither to the biblical texts nor to the depressing reality of the gay subculture that he had moved in and out of for twenty years."[1]

Hays writes that he and Gary were frustrated that:

"The public discussion of this matter has been dominated by insistently ideological voices; on one side, gay rights activists demanding the church's unqualified acceptance of homosexuality; on the other, unqualified homophobic condemnation of homosexual Christians. [2]

Gary died shortly after his visit. Hays wrote his article in hope that it would foster compassionate and careful theological reflection within the community of faith. It is with this same desire and in the same spirit that I attempt to reflect on this strongly emotional and sensitive issue. This book is written with the Garys in our churches in mind.

The third group in mind in this writing is those men and women who have fully embraced their homosexuality. Few of these persons wanted this orientation. Their discovery that they might be homosexual brought feelings of fear, dismay and anxiety. For some, pain was increased by ill-treatment or outright condemnation by misinformed people. But they have worked at getting through those feelings of bewilderment and pain and have become accepting of who they are. They perceive that the origin of their homosexuality is genetic. They are convinced that they are born that way – that they are a distinct creation. These homosexual persons believe that just as Afro-Americans cannot determine the color of their skin, neither can homosexuals determine their orientation. It follows that if their homosexuality is genetic, it cannot be changed.

Those who make up this third group cannot understand why there should be any debate at all on the subject.

Since homosexuality is innate and fixed they believe that gay and lesbian persons should be afforded full civil rights. They insist that the church accept homosexuals as equal to heterosexuals in every respect. Same-sex unions of trust and fidelity should be affirmed and blessed, non-celibate homosexual pastors should be ordained by the same standards as straight persons, lesbigay parents should be accorded adoption rights, equal rights should be accorded in the courts, and homosexuality should be celebrated as part of God's good creation.

In the pages that follow, we will look at the scientific support for this view of homosexuality. We will see where the scientific world weighs in on this matter. We will listen to the voice of science as it addresses the foundational claim that homosexuals are a distinct creation, a claim which in turn has shaped the beliefs and views that are built on that foundation.

Part I is devoted to understanding in broad strokes the homosexual condition. Listening, learning, and gaining accurate information is the essential starting point for one wanting to become informed. The reader will quickly learn that the homosexual phenomenon is an extremely complex matter. This section addresses four popular myths. It looks at   what the most recent research in the area of biology and the social sciences is saying about causation. It speaks to what homosexuals do and the gay agenda for society and church.

Part II seeks to answer the question, "Is homosexuality contrary to the will of God?" We will look at the Bible's teaching regarding homosexual behavior and particularly the debate among Christians as to what the Bible teaches. This section is introduced by corollary discussions regarding the authority of Scripture in the homosexual debate and the task of interpreting the biblical texts under discussion. It concludes with an analysis of four of the most common analogies used in the homosexual debate taking place within the church today.

Part III formulates a response to the question, "What is to be the church's attitude toward homosexual persons?" Many homosexual persons have been deeply wounded by the church's attitudes. The work of the Holy Spirit in the life of the church to enable Christians in our day to express Christian love and humility and compassion is examined. We explore the call upon the churches to be environments of hope, acceptance, grace, forgiveness, and healing. Finally, within the call to speak the truth in love, we address the issues of church discipline and the pressing questions of whether or not to bless same-sex unions and ordain practicing homosexuals.

What follows is an attempt to address these critical questions facing the church today from within the setting of the local church and to search for answers which are consistent with the Scriptures and historic Christianity.

Part 1
# Understanding Homosexuality

# ONE
## Four Common Myths

Through the years, certain people have come into my life with whom I have developed a friendship beyond that of just a pastor-church member relationship. Within the dynamics of that friendship, I then learned that they were struggling with homosexual feelings and behavior. Perhaps that has been God's way of keeping me from becoming homophobic, from having a fear of homosexuals. But those times of disclosure have been moments of truth for me. Knowing that this friend is struggling in this area, does this man, this homosexual, does this woman, this lesbian still matter to me? Does it change the nature of our friendship? Does this man or this woman still matter to God?

In the fall of 2002, I delivered an extended series of sermons on contemporary social and moral issues facing the church. I did so out of the strong conviction that the Lord of the Church calls local churches and individual Christ followers to be salt and light in society. There were 12 messages in the series - yes 12! - which addressed chemical addiction, human sexuality, divorce and remarriage, pornography, abortion, racism and poverty. Two of the messages spoke to the matter of homosexuality. The entire list of sermon titles, texts, and dates was published in the weekly worship folder and monthly newsletter prior to the start of the series so everyone could see what would be coming. As the series began, without question, more than regarding any other topic, people came to me and said, "Dave, I'm really looking forward to the sermons on homosexuality." It was obvious that it was an issue many wanted to learn more about.

In recent years, more and more of us have come to know gay and lesbian persons. More and more of us have friends, co-workers, family members, and fellow church members who are homosexual. We have become much more aware of homosexual persons around us. There are some of us who are struggling with homosexual thoughts, feelings, and behaviors ourselves. People are talking more openly about their sexuality. There is a concerted effort to portray the homosexual lifestyle as widespread and normal, a perfectly acceptable lifestyle. Homosexuality is being hotly debated at the national, state, and local levels of government, on our college and university campuses, and in major church denominations. Television shows have been overrun with homosexual characters. Homosexuality is here and it is not going away. As one lesbian author has written, "We are everywhere".[1]

For the Christian Church there are two major questions: "Is homosexuality contrary to the will of God?" and "What is to be the Church's attitude toward homosexuals?" Church denominations are trying to craft responses for their people that will not blow their churches apart. As I am writing this I am in Wales. Next door in England, 38 primates of the worldwide Anglican Communion are preparing to gather in London to discuss how to head off a looming split over homosexuality. They may or may not be successful. I hope and pray they are.

But where the answers to these two questions must be lived out and practiced is at the corner of Mississippi Street and East River Road or near County Road B and Highway 10 where you and I live out our Sunday through Saturday lives. Denominational social policy statements may have their value and place. I believe they do. But there are not only real issues at stake here. The lives of real people are at risk. The real issue is how do I minister to Collin, one of my most faithful Sunday School teachers, who tells me, his pastor, that he has been living with a gay partner for two years? Or what are we to say to Judy who shared with our small group last night that she is in a lesbian relationship? What do the Scriptures say to Collin? What attitude is the church to have toward Judy?

To begin with, definitions and terminology are important. By "homosexuality" or "homosexual orientation" we mean a preference for persons of the same sex involving erotic attraction. By "homosexual behavior" we are referring to the physical expression of this attraction. It is important to note that a person can have a homosexual orientation without ever engaging in homosexual behavior and that a person can engage in homosexual behavior without having a homosexual orientation. While these descriptions are helpful and necessary, we at the same time acknowledge that human experience is tremendously diverse and that people and acts in this sexual area are not easily classified.

The place to begin formulating a response to the two questions regarding the morality of homosexual behavior and our attitude toward homosexual persons is with understanding. Though we are confronted more and more on every side by homosexuality, few of us really know much about this whole subject. In the two sermons to the congregation on homosexuality, this is where I began. The people's eager anticipation of these particular messages in the series indicated to me that they wanted to listen and learn and become informed. I have learned that fears of homosexuality are best overcome by gaining accurate information. I felt it important to begin by dispelling four of the most common myths with respect to homosexuality.

**The first myth is the myth of the ten percent.** "Ten percent of the adult population is homosexual" is a statistic that has become a normal part of America's vocabulary. We hear the ten percent figure repeated over and over again in the press, radio, and television. The prevalence estimate appears frequently in scientific and professional literature. It also appears frequently in the moral debate in church documents on human sexuality. In a debate between the liberal Episcopal bishop John Spong and the conservative leaning Episcopal bishop John Howe, Spong emphasized the 10% figure, declaring that only narrow-minded conservatives would even bother to question the figure.[2] But does the evidence argue for this 10% figure? How common is homosexuality in America?

The 10% figure is inextricably tied to the famous Kinsey studies. Alfred Kinsey was an entomologist (a researcher of insects) at the University of Indiana who, in the 1940s and 1950s, chose to turn his scientific interest away from his primary field of training to the topic of human sexuality. In James Jones' biography of Kinsey, *Alfred C. Kinsey: a Public/Private Life,* the author tells of a deeply troubled man, a masochist and closet homosexual, who was obsessed with sex and driven by his own sexual demons to liberate people from the grips of Victorian repression. Jones says that Kinsey's guiding light was sexual liberation, not science.[3]

In 1948 Kinsey published *Sexual Behavior in the Human Male* and in 1953 *Sexual Behavior in the Human Female*. In these massive volumes Kinsey's message is that "everyone is doing it, so it must be normal".[4] People have since extrapolated from this argument that whatever is statistical is normal and right. Kinsey's two studies came to be seen as the scientific bedrock of the sexual revolution of the 1960's and the homosexual revolution that has followed. In the first study Kinsey estimated that 4% of white American males were exclusively homosexual throughout their lives after adolescence, 10% were practicing homosexuals during at least a three-year period between the ages of 16 and 55, and 37% have some incidental homosexual experience at some time during their lives. In his study of female sexuality, he reported that female homosexuality appeared to occur at about half the rate of male homosexuality. If you translate these figures, this means that about 1 in 25 adult males and about 1 in 45 adult females are exclusively homosexual in orientation.

The 10% figure is usually attributed to the Kinsey report on males and is used to justify the prevalence of homosexuality in America. In light of this fact, we note that Kinsey reported a range of different statistics on homosexual behavior. It comes as a surprise to many that Kinsey *never* reported that 10% of the population is homosexual as is often suggested in popular reports or discussions. He said that 4% are exclusively homosexual throughout their lives and that 10% are exclusively homosexual during a three-year period. The 10% figure took on a life of its own. The figure was not publicly or widely called into question until the early 1990s. One of its first indictments was a *Time* magazine article published on April 26, 1993 entitled "The Shrinking Ten Percent." In the article the author, Priscilla Painton, made reference to a major national survey which found that only 1% of the 3,321 men surveyed considered themselves exclusively homosexual.

Kinsey's data appears to be deeply flawed. Upon publication of his two studies, critiques were made of both his methodology and conclusions, but the wind of liberation had caught the imagination of the public. This public mood had been conditioned by a subtle but widespread disenchantment with the biblical foundations of western civilization. It was in this mileau that the pansexual revolution began to gain momentum. The critiques of Kinsey's work went largely unheeded in the media for the next three decades. But then in 1990, Edward Eichel and Judith Reisman published *Kinsey, Sex, and Fraud.* Their book documents the deceit and fraudulence behind Kinsey's statistics and in addition exposes his (or his helpers') criminal abuse of children from infancy into teens in order to get his "scientific" data.[5]

With regard to Kinsey's methodology and his statistics regarding homosexuality, it needs to be pointed out that "for a study such as Kinsey's to produce data from which we could generalize to the whole population, the sample under study would have to be roughly representative of the general population".[6] There are striking examples of groups sampled by Kinsey that were not representative of the general population. For example, Kinsey over sampled college students who are more likely to have engaged in "unusual" sexual practices than the non college population. He over sampled Protestants at the expense of Catholics who were less likely to have engaged in "unusual" sexual practices. He over sampled prison inmates and adding insult to injury, he especially sought interviews with sex offenders, men imprisoned for such crimes as pederasty (child molestation), rape, and sodomy (homosexual behavior). Kinsey over sampled members of gay-affirming organizations, recruiting subjects from homosexual friendship and acquaintance networks in big cities.[7] These samples can hardly be seen as groups that are truly representative of the population as a whole.

In recent years, many credible studies have been published which give us a much more accurate insight into how common homosexuality actually is in America. Every serious study since Kinsey, both in America and abroad, has made clear that the homosexual population is somewhere in the 1-3% range.[8]

In their excellent book, *Homosexuality: The Use of Scientific Research in the Church's Moral Debate*, Jones and Yarhouse look at the research in detail. These studies are united in telling us that the prevalence of homosexuality is significantly less that those reported by Kinsey and promoted by others—including those promoting change in the church. At the conclusion of a chapter entitled "How Prevalent is Homosexuality?" Jones and Yarhouse summarize the most recent credible research on homosexuality:[8]

• The infamous "10% of the population is gay" pronouncement has been consistently shown to be based on a misinterpretation of deeply flawed research published by Kinsey.

• More recent and more credible studies suggest that less than 3%, and perhaps less than 2%, of males are homosexually active in a given year.

• Probably fewer than 5% of the adult male population engage in sustained homosexual practice over a significant period of adult life.

• Female homosexuality is estimated at approximately half or less than the male rates and appears to characterize less than 2% of the female population.

• Combining males and females, homosexuality almost certainly characterizes less than 3% (and perhaps less than 2%) of the population.

The myth of the 10% has survived far too long. It is time to expose it and in light of the evidence bury it.

**The second myth is that homosexuals are born that way.** You have undoubtedly heard this one over and over and over again. In recent years the popular media has confidently proclaimed that scientists have reached a definite conclusion about sexual orientation. "There is a gay gene responsible for it," they say. In her column Ann Landers repeatedly affirms that homosexuals are born not made. Leading up to the 2004 Iowa caucuses, one of the presidential candidates was quoted in the Washington Post that God must have thought homosexuality was not a sin because He created "gay" people. And so we are led to believe that such a discovery is an established scientific fact. In my reading on the subject, I find it stated or implied time and time again. As a result this myth is widely believed.

The Gay Liberation Movement and the Christian Homophile Movement aggressively spread this myth. They say, "We've been born this way," or "God made us this way. It is in our genetic makeup. We cannot change our genetics." It is claimed that just as some people are born left-handed or brown-eyed, certain people are born homosexual. Since homosexuality is genetic, it is no longer a question of responsibility or fault. Homosexuality must be accepted by everyone as an alternative lifestyle. But is this contention a responsible way of dealing with the scientific evidence?

In preparing for the sermon series and since, I have spent a significant amount of time reading and researching the literature and listening to the stories and experiences of homosexual persons. I have read major books and countless magazine and newspaper articles and periodicals. In all this reading and research, I have not been able to find one conclusive documented scientific study that substantiates the hypothesis that homosexuals are born that way. On the contrary, there is a consensus among geneticists who state that there is no firm basis for believing that homosexuality is genetically determined.

On July 15, 1993, National Public Radio reported a new study in *Science* magazine celebrating the so-called discovery of the gene that causes homosexuality. The discovery, it was stated, had been made by Dean Hamer, a molecular biologist, and others at the National Cancer Institute. Near the end of the broadcast, the necessary qualifiers were quickly added, but most people would have turned off their radio saying, "There it is. Homosexuality is caused by a gene!" Many still believe so.

But has a gay gene in fact been discovered? Even the *New York Times* immediately warned people against over-interpreting the work. Four months later, genetics researchers from Yale, Columbia and Louisiana State University wrote a critical commentary pointing out that the study was seriously flawed. Following this criticism, Dean Hamer, a self-proclaimed homosexual, came under investigation by the Office of Research Integrity at the Department of Health and Human Services for selectively reporting his data. He was brought up on charges by a fellow research assistant who alleged that Hamer withheld some of the findings that would have invalidated his study. A Canadian research team using a similar experimental design was unable to duplicate Hamer's findings. Hamer himself has since declared, "These genes do not cause people to become homosexual . . . the biology or personality is much more complicated than that."[10] It would seem fair and right if NPR would have reported this part of the story as well.

Contrary to much popular opinion, no "gay gene" has been identified up to this time. Most geneticists now believe that if the cause(s) of homosexuality is ever determined, it will be a much more complex matter than a single genetic factor. But for years now, a great deal of energy and research has been taking place in an attempt to so identify causal factors. It seems responsible and safe to say that if scientists really had identified a gay gene responsible for homosexual orientation, respected researchers who want to establish a biological basis for sexual orientation would not be spending such enormous amounts of time or energy or finances trying to establish a biological link through research.[11]

Even gay-activist researchers who themselves have been desperately searching for a genetic element to homosexuality have openly admitted their failure to do so. According to Dean Hamer, "There is not a single master gene that makes people gay. . . I don't think we will ever be able to predict who will be gay."[12] Simon LeVay, a neuroanatomist and gay-activist researcher who became well-known after researching and publishing the study of hypothalamic structures in men most widely-cited as confirming innate brain differences between homosexuals and heterosexuals, commenting on his work says, "I did not prove that homosexuality is genetic, or find a genetic cause for being gay. I didn't show that gay men are born that way, the most common mistake people make in interpreting my work."[13] Lesbian philosopher and activist Camille Paglia is quite blunt in her assessment of the "born gay" theory. "No one is born gay. The idea is ridiculous . . . homosexuality is an adaptation, not an inborn trait."[14]

I think it would be accurate to speculate that if in fact there is a gay gene and it has been discovered in some laboratory somewhere in the world, the gay activists would be purchasing one page ads in every major newspaper in the country. They would be on every network and cable television channel. Articles and books would be written and published which document the discovery. It would be the biggest news story of the year! It would be the 'smoking gun' of the gay movement. The reason they have not done these things is because no gay gene has been discovered.

**A third myth is that homosexuals lead happy lives.** This myth is so widespread that I would guess a majority of people believe it. Why would they think otherwise? Will on *Will & Grace* is a well adjusted, funny, and happy guy. We see 45-second clips on TV where young men are holding hands with each other and young women are strolling arm in arm with each other and kissing one another and parading through the streets of Chicago and New York and San Francisco and they look happy. After all, they are called "gay" aren't they?

But this myth covers up a human tragedy. Things are not always as they appear. It is, of course, possible to paint a picture of a homosexual couple that glows with the *claims* of joy and happiness. And that picture may be a reality for certain homosexual couples. That must be acknowledged. But regarding the majority the question needs to be asked concerning the quality and the permanence of that 'joy'. Ill-advised behavior is not unknown to produce pleasure and feelings of happiness and well being. The New Testament, indeed, says, *"There is pleasure in sin for a season."* (Hebrews 11:25) There are fleeting pleasures in many areas of conduct and life. While it is undoubtedly true that homosexual persons deeply long for intimacy and permanence in relationships, it is nonetheless commonly known that one of the distinguishing marks of homosexual relationships is impermanence. This leads one to ask, "How permanent is homosexual joy?" As one psychiatrist has put it, "The fact remains that the gay world is far from as gay as it is named."[15]

The reality for many people is that the homosexual experience is one of pain. I could hear the pain as a woman who had been living in a lesbian relationship for ten years confided to me in the privacy of my office, "Who would choose to be gay?" It is not as it appears. The truth be told, of the 1-3 million homosexuals in this country, only a fraction would say they are fulfilled or happy in their orientation and lifestyle. The overwhelming majority would give anything not to be gay. The gay life as a whole is not gay. Why? There may be many reasons, but the reality is that fear is a significant characteristic that grips the lives of homosexual persons.

*Homosexual persons live with the fear of being found out.* To live with a secret that one is afraid to share with others is a lonely, lonely life. How will my friends react if they find out? Will they still accept me? Will my parents still love me? What untold pain and sorrow will I cause my family when they are told? Will my church turn their back on me?

*Homosexual persons live in fear of contracting sexually transmitted diseases.* Studies are telling us that over the course of a lifetime, many homosexuals will have over 1000 sexual encounters with men.[16] It is less for lesbians who have fewer casual episodes or sexual encounters. One doctor has said that with that kind of sexual interaction, an active homosexual has a 365% greater chance of getting a sexually transmitted disease than a heterosexual. We are aware of how the threat of AIDS has spread in recent years. Although the virus is transmitted by heterosexual as well as homosexual intercourse, a part of the reason why the wider community ought to be concerned about homosexuality is because it is not just a moral issue anymore. It is that but it is more. It is a public safety issue because more and more people are carrying the AIDS virus and working in positions where the spread of the infection is possible.

*Homosexual persons live in fear of violence.* The fear spoken of here is not that of straight people being violent against gay people. Yes, to be sure, there are the exceptions like the well known and highly publicized tragic death of Matthew Shepherd. That is an atrocity that all must speak out against. But that is not what is meant here. Few gays are afraid of being treated violently by heterosexuals. Homosexuals are afraid of being turned on, beaten, and subjected to deviant sexual behavior by other homosexuals with whom they are having sexual encounters. Gay-on-gay violence is the secret homosexuals don't like to confront. Yet they know that violence against one another is a major problem. According to two homosexual activists who have written a book several inches thick on the subject, "We believe as many as 650,000 gay men may be victims of domestic violence each year in the United States".[17] The potential for abuse is greatest in the area of sexuality because of the addictive character of sexual pleasure. The research says that the intensity of homosexual desire is unbelievable. We who are heterosexual have strong lusts now and then. From what I am told, heterosexual lust is not as intense as homosexual lust.

*Homosexual persons live in fear of aging.* As one despairing homosexual put it, "Who wants an old faggot?" The poster child of the gay movement in popular culture is the well-built, physically fit young man. But young men grow into old men who are no longer physically desirable. After years of homosexual activity, what does an aged, undesirable homosexual have to look forward to? The reality is they are often subjugated to the most heinous and devious forms of sexual activity such as sadomasochism, humiliation, defecation, and urination. We would do well to remember also that there is no spouse to come home to. There are no grandchildren around the footstool. There are no white picket fences within which to face the end years of life. For so many homosexuals, growing old is a dark road that gets darker with each passing year. In light of this reality, it perhaps is not surprising to read of a high incidence of depression and a high suicide rate among homosexuals.

*Some homosexual persons live in fear of God.* Many homosexuals have been so thoroughly deceived and have such seared consciences that they have no conscious awareness that they will give an account of their lives before a holy God one day. But a vast majority in the homosexual community still have a memory from somewhere in their past that God has forbidden the practice of homosexual acts and that He will not tolerate sin. Some fear that God hates them. So they live with the foreboding Sword of Damocles hanging by a thread over their heads. Life isn't gay in the gay community.

**A fourth myth is that homosexuals cannot change.** This myth says there is no hope that things can be different. The Gay Movement says very strongly that once you are gay it is a waste of time to try to change. It believes that any fundamental change is very difficult if not impossible. You will drive yourself crazy trying to change, they say. The assertion is made that for some people homosexuality is as natural as left-handedness. Surely, they say, God would not condemn people for an orientation that cannot be changed.

I am going to ask the heterosexuals who are reading this to do something with me. Would you put yourselves for a few moments in the shoes of a homosexual person? The earliest memories you have of your childhood is that "I was not like other boys." All you know is that you are different and strange—and you don't know why. You just are. Growing up in your family through adolescence and young adulthood, you surmise that you were born that way. You were ostracized and rejected and ridiculed and intimidated by the opposite sex. Somewhere along the way you were seduced by someone of the same sex. It was a highly erotic experience that eventually became a pattern in your life. You live with an incredible amount of fear and a boatload of guilt. You fear being sent to hell. You are facing a bleak and lonely future. The threat of AIDS lurks in the back of your consciousness the older you get.

Is it any wonder so many homosexual persons are despondent and paranoid and overcome by feelings of hopelessness? Someone has told you that your homosexuality is genetic. You believe it because it seems to fit your experience. If you are genetically determined, then there is nothing you or anyone else can do to change it. It is who you are. Your only sexual desires are for persons of the same sex. You must accept it and live with it and know that there can never be a change in the course of your life.

Putting yourselves in the shoes of such a one perhaps does for you what it has done for me. In my interaction with homosexual persons and in my study and reading, I have developed an enormous amount of compassion (I know that will be taken by some as patronizing) for homosexuals. I may not condone their behavior. But I can empathize with their plight and agony. They matter to me and even more, they matter to God.

*Is there hope of change for a homosexual?* Biblical teaching, scientific studies and human experience all have answered that question in the affirmative. The Bible tells us there is a way out for homosexuals—at least a way out of homosexual behavior. The central message of the Bible is one of hope. It tells us that what is impossible for us is possible for God. It tells us that we can do things we never thought we could with God's help. The Bible tells us that the risen and living Christ is available to us now and that he is greater than forces that act upon us.

With specific regard to homosexuality, Paul in I Corinthians 6 gives a long list of sins which include those identified as "male prostitutes" and "sodomites." Paul is saying that some of the Corinthian Christians once had been involved in homosexual practice but that they no longer are so involved. Christ had been preached and met them and washed them in forgiveness and justified them and through the Holy Spirit they were being sanctified. They had been delivered and changed and had stopped their homosexual sin. The Bible's message is one of hope. Through the workings and power of the Holy Spirit in a person's life, there is hope for change for the homosexual.

We also look to the witness of scientific studies that change is possible. During the 1960s, 1970s, and mid-1980s, there were successes reported by the psychoanalytic forms of treatment (with a shift toward research on biological theories in the late 1980s and 1990s).[18] But there are limits and problems as well. When a doctor, who is not part of the man's world, sees the man at most once or twice a week and whose task it is to counteract the influences that press upon him at home, at his work and leisure, in fact throughout his waking hours, there may indeed be limited progress. However, even from early on significant success was recorded.

In 1962 Dr. Irving Bieber reported 27% success with his psychoanalytical methods. In 1967 Feldman and MacCulloch reported 58% success with their adversative techniques. These and other successes lead John Court to write, "It is now possible to refute categorically the view that the homosexual condition cannot be effectively treated".[19] Masters and Johnson, the famed sex researchers, report a 50-60% improvement or cure rate for highly motivated clients.[20] Charles Socarides, a Fellow of the American Psychiatric Association and a Clinical Professor of Psychiatry at the Albert Einstein College of Medicine in New York, reported a success rate of almost 50% in achieving full heterosexual functioning.[21] Jeffrey Satinover, former Fellow in Psychiatry and Child Psychiatry at Yale University, reports a 52% success rate in the treatment of unwanted homosexual attraction.[22] Other professionals report success rates ranging from 30% to 79%. It is not that change is easy and there are varying degrees of change. There is hope but it must be tempered with realism. It is very unlikely, for example, that an older, exclusively homosexual man who is in any way pressured into treatment will benefit from treatment.

More recently, in May 2001, Dr. Robert Spitzer, the prominent psychiatrist and researcher at Columbia University, presented a new study to the American Psychiatric Association which suggested that persons who desire to change their sexual orientation can do so with success. Spitzer's study revealed 200 men and women who have experienced a significant shift from homosexual to heterosexual attraction and have sustained this change for at least five years.

Spitzer was the chief decision-maker in the 1973 American Psychiatric Association decision that removed homosexuality from the official diagnostic manual of mental disorders. He considers himself a gay-affirmative psychiatrist and a long time supporter of gay rights. Now, says Spitzer, his views on homosexuality have changed. "Like most psychiatrists, I thought that homosexual behavior could only be resisted, and that no one could really change their sexual orientation. I now believe that to be false. Some people can and do change."[23] Dr. Joseph Nicolosi, president of the National Association for Research and Therapy of Homosexuality (NARTH), noted, "Dr. Spitzer's study found that 67 percent of the men who had rarely or never felt any opposite sex attraction before the change effort now report significant heterosexual attraction."[24]

What is intriguing was Dr. Spitzer's reply to a journalist who asked what he would do if his own adolescent son revealed a homosexual attraction. Dr. Spitzer responded by saying he would hope his son would be interested in changing and would get some help. It is worthy of note that when Dr. Spitzer presented his results to the Gay and Lesbian committees of the APA, anticipating a scientific debate, he was shocked to be met with intense pressure to withhold his findings for political reasons. Dr. Spitzer has received considerable "hate mail" and complaints from his colleagues on account of his research.[25]

But at this point I wanted to be completely honest about this myth with the congregation as I spoke to them that Sunday morning. Especially I had in mind individuals in the congregation who were struggling with homosexual desires and behavior. I explained to them that along with the hope that God's Word instills comes the sobering reality that change may and probably will be a long, difficult, and painful challenge. Indeed, there are wonderful stories of homosexual persons being miraculously delivered and healed by the direct intervention of the Holy Spirit, not only from homosexual behavior, but thoughts and feelings as well. I rejoice when I hear of God's Spirit working this powerful way. Yet, even Christian ministries attempting to help the homosexual change, many represented by the umbrella Exodus International organization, generally agree that change is a difficult and painful process involving repentance, renouncing attitudes, and embracing God's promises.

These ministries find that individuals who are being successful in their attempts at sexual reorientation, or at least sexual control, seem to hold three values in common:

*First, a strong unswerving commitment to Jesus Christ.* Without a strong belief in Christ, they rarely see progress in the life of a homosexual struggling for wholeness. Many homosexuals who are finding their way to sexual health have devoted themselves to Christ in a tenacious and extraordinary way.

*Second, there is the establishment of a long-term relationship with a professional therapist.* Even if there is miraculous release from feelings, desires, and behavior, there are those early family dynamics that need to be understood and unraveled and worked through. Ceasing from homosexual contacts will not abolish the emotional needs that led to them in the first place. Learned psychological and emotional patterns have to be sifted through. There is the anger and self hatred and rejection that need to be faced. There is a huge amount of effort that awaits the homosexual who wants out of his lifestyle. But it is a work that will bring release and freedom.

*Third, there is an accepting environment in which progress and healing toward sexual wholeness can be made.* This is the question for our churches that we turn to in the last section of this book. Can our churches be the kind of communities that offer a supportive, understanding environment in which people can struggle for wholeness in this sexual area? It is my strong conviction that life change is more likely to take place through interaction within a caring, supportive community, than in the isolated setting of the psychiatrist's couch.

If the truth be known, every one of us is battling something—greed, envy, lust, pride, loneliness, drug addiction, alcohol addiction, pornography addiction, fear—some of us homosexuality. In these daily struggles we are not as different from one another as we may think. There is hope for us all! I do not think it is too strong to say that the only hope for any of us—including the homosexual—is Jesus Christ and the loving, accepting, caring community of his church. We will speak more of this later.

# TWO
## Causes of Homosexuality

So what causes homosexuality if it is not genetically determined? Faced with this question we must immediately admit the obvious. The entire homosexual phenomenon is a terribly complex matter. Bright minds have been trying for years to better understand its roots and causes. Even the most recent research has not given us a definitive answer.

Daniel Olson, professor of pastoral care at Wartburg Theological Seminary, Dubuque, Iowa, has looked at the research published since the turn of the new millennium. He finds that between January 2000 and June 2002, more than 600 research articles about sexual orientation were published in scientific journals of biology, neuroscience, psychology, and the social sciences. He reports that as of June 2002, scientists still do not know what causes homosexuality.[1] Even after years of observation and study, then, if you ask an honest researcher the simple question "What causes homosexuality?" the truthful response will be "We are not really sure. We still don't know". But if one presses these knowledgeable experts as to what they *think* might be contributing factors, they will say there is considerable evidence pointing to at least three contributing factors.

### Early Family Relationships

The first factor is **negative dynamics in early relationships in family life.** These negative influences create certain kinds of pressures that first send young children down the path of developing a homosexual vulnerability, and then later, a homosexual orientation if some other things happen.

A few years ago, I was asked to conduct a funeral service for a young homosexual man. He was the friend of an acquaintance of mine. In light of my studies and interest, I was curious about this young man's family background. When meeting with my friend and a few of the young man's relatives, I simply asked them to reflect on his early family life. I learned that here again was one whose early life profile was characterized by destructive family dynamics. It is cause for weeping. Time after time the stories are so similar.

The picture that emerges with regard to a large number of persons with strong homosexual tendencies is fairly similar. A father in the home is not particularly interested in or loving and approving of his son and is sometimes overly critical and hostile. Or the father had a low status in the family and tended to be weak when compared with the mother. The mother in the home tended to be over protective of her son. She was the prominent disciplinarian in the home. She also tended to be jealous of the sexual development of her son, restricting his heterosexual contacts and development. The relationship between the parents tended to be poor and the child tended to be isolated from his male peers. He tended to be quiet, introverted, sometimes described as effeminate. And the first experience of erotic arousal in adolescence was usually with another boy or man.

There are many factors but one striking theme is that the thing lacking in these boys' lives is the pre-adolescent relationship with the parent of the same sex.[2] The father is not a good role model in that he is largely absent or very critical and rejecting of his son. As a result there isn't the opportunity for identification as a man and approval from a man. So the boy is arrested in his emotional growth at that stage and when he gets into adolescence, he starts to look for the sort of things he wanted and needed from his father—affirmation, identification, and approval. He finds it, but now the problem as an adolescent is that his physiology has moved on. He is now erotically aroused by close physical contact.

With women the picture is not as clear. There was often a poor relationship with the mother and a fair relationship with the father. But there was a high incidence of a loss of parents or of parental discord, that is, fighting and drinking. The girls tended to be described as Tom-boys.

So if there hasn't been this relationship with a father or a girl with her mother in the pre-adolescent period, as they reach adolescence they are pulled into other relationships as they seek for approval, security, and identity as a man or as a woman. There can, of course, be several other kinds of combinations that can result in sexual and psychological confusion. But notice that in these combinations there is a negative dynamic with the same-sex parent.

Dr. George Rekers is an expert on Gender Identity Disorders and has authored dozens of scholarly research papers on homosexuality. In 1982 he authored *Growing Up Straight: What Every Family Should Know About Homosexuality.* He is also editor of *Handbook of Child and Adolescent Sexual Problems* published in 1995. Dr. Reders has stated:

"Gender nonconformity in childhood may be the single common observable factor associated with homosexuality. Some of the typical childhood factors leading to homosexuality are: feeling of being different from other children; perception of father as being distant, uninvolved and unapproving; perception of mother being too close, too involved; diminished or distorted masculinity or femininity; premature introduction to sexuality; and gender confusion."[3]

Dr. Joseph Nicolosi, president of the National Association for Research and Therapy of Homosexuality has written:

"Homosexuality is a development problem that is almost always the result of problems in family relationships, particularly between father and son. As a result of failure with father, the boy does not fully internalize male gender identity, and develops homosexuality. This is the most commonly seen clinical model."[4]

Counselors who work in this field tell us that it is not uncommon for boys between the ages of 8 and 14 to go through a period of confused sexual feelings. It is a window of time during which they are asking, "What is masculinity? What is femininity? What is sexuality?" If this is indeed the case, then one immediately can think of possible scenarios. Shane is a normal, impressionable young boy who, in that critical window of development, is trying to make sense of his sexual feelings. During this time there is shaming going on within the family. He has anger raging within against his father. There are people around him adding to his gender confusion. You have the emotional and psychological seed-bed that can develop into a homosexual vulnerability and orientation.

What must be stated very carefully at this point is that this is not to suggest that early destructive family dynamics is the only or even necessarily the greatest contributing factor to the development of homosexuality. It is an extremely complex thing. There are some homosexuals who have no such family background factors. There are others who have only one or two factors. But there does appear to be a great deal of evidence which argues that destructive family dynamics certainly seem to make someone more vulnerable to becoming homosexual.

### Early Homosexual Experience

A second contributing factor is **early homosexual experiences with a trusted friend or family member.** Adolescence is an extremely impressionable time. During that sexually confusing time in the developmental window, Uncle Steven or Cousin Eddie from down the street steps into the scene and enlightens Johnny to the thrills and chills of sexual expression! When a vulnerable young boy or girl participates in a powerful sexual activity with a trusted friend or family member of the same sex, the consequences can be lasting. Add into the mix the strong desire to escape from a raging father or a controlling mother and the addictive power of sex, a direction can begin to be established.

So a young man may go out in his early teen years not looking for sex but just for affection and affirmation from another man which he never had. His first sexual encounter may be with an older man who just befriends him. But this young man who is developing sexually may very quickly get involved in a sexual relationship if the older man takes advantage. Such an initial sexual experience can be very important in shaping a young man's identity.[5] Now again, it is not just the sexual experience. It is the sexual experience in the context of a cluster of relational and emotional and psychological factors that are present.

In 1985 and 1988, Robert Johnson and Diana Shrier conducted research studies which found that males who had been sexually abused as children were almost seven times as likely as non-molested boys to become homosexuals.[6] Dr. Gregory Dickinson conducted a study which revealed that 49% of homosexuals surveyed had been molested compared to less than 2% of heterosexuals. His study affirms previous findings of Dr. David Finkelhor which found that boys victimized by older men were four times more likely to be currently involved in homosexual behaviors than were non-victims. As Finkelhor observed:

"It may be common for a boy who has been involved in an experience with an older man to label himself as homosexual because he has had a homosexual experience and because he was found to be sexually attractive by a man. Once he labels himself homosexual, the boy may begin to behave consistently with the role and gravitate toward homosexual activity."[7]

Dr. Robert Hicks, counselor and author of *The Masculine Journey* has written:

"In counseling gay men for twenty years, I have not had one yet whom I would say had a normative childhood or normative adolescent development in the sexual arena. More often than not I have found stories of abusive, alcoholic, or absent (physically and emotionally) fathers: stories of incest or first experiences of sex forced upon them by older brothers, neighborhood men, or even friends."[8]

### Genetic Predisposition

A third contributing factor is **the influence of genetic predisposition.** This factor is the most difficult to substantiate concretely but there seems to be substantial evidence for it. There are studies on identical twins in particular which have demonstrated that there may well be some genetic predisposition. Many scientists share the view that sexual orientation is shaped for most people at an early age through complex interactions of biological, psychological and social factors. The point has been strongly made above that no gay gene has been discovered. But just as there is the possibility of a genetic predisposition or vulnerability to alcohol which contributes to alcoholism, there does appear to be a genetic predisposition toward homosexuality. Whitehead, a scientist who studied the influence of genetic predisposition, estimates a 10% influence on a person becoming homosexual.[8] These same scientists point out, however, that there are genetic components in virtually everything we do but that these are not decisive. We may be genetically influenced but we are not genetically determined. Our genes don't force us to do anything. We are not machines but rather significant human beings who have the ability to make responsible choices along life's way.

Jeffrey Satinover, who has practiced psychoanalysis and psychiatry with homosexuals for more than 20 years, summarizes well the extreme complexity of the matter:

> "Like all behavioral and mental states, homosexuality is multifactorial. It is neither biological nor exclusively psychological, but results from an as-yet-difficult-to-quantify mixture of genetic factors, intrauterine influences, postnatal environment, and a complex series of repeatedly reinforced choices occurring at critical phases of development."[10]

William Byne and Bruce Parsons of Columbia University have called this the 'interactionist model' which seems to do justice to the complexity of the human being. We are a cluster of our biology, our physiology, our hormones and our social relationships. We are each different and unique individuals influenced by different combinations of these many factors. With one homosexual person it may be a certain amount of genetic predisposition. With another it will be the family relationships. In a third it will be the teaching about sex in their family. In still another it may be the attitudes in the church about sex mixed in with the family relationships. A person then gets involved in a homosexual relationship which—especially if you are a Christian—brings on the cycles of self-hatred, guilt and shame. How then do you deal with guilt and shame? Very often you suppress it. You push it down inside and seek comfort and intimacy from another person or from a drug or something to dull the pain. This leads to getting caught up in even more cycles of negative, destructive behavior. Given these combinations plus our own sinful tendencies to lust, pride, envy, self-centeredness, self-gratification and rebellion which need somehow to be separated out and dealt with in terms of repentance—well, you put that in a pot and stew it together and you have a pretty potent cocktail!

But with specific regard for the genetic and biological research that has been referred to, that research does not affect the morality of the situation. What *is* does not always tell us what *ought to be.* What we find in ourselves does not tell us what we ought to be. We cannot tell from the genes, the anatomy or the chemistry whether this was part of the Creator's intent or a disorder which is a result of the Fall. If there is a genetic predisposition to alcoholism, and many scientists believe there is a predisposition involved, we do not assume this is a good thing or that people with this propensity should not or cannot be at least to some degree held responsible for their behavior. If there is a genetic endowment to violence, let's say child-battering, we would say that responsibility has perhaps diminished but at the same time we would say the act is wrong and sinful and consider it something to be prevented. It would be the same if there were to be a genetic disposition to anger or overeating. We would not assume this to be a good thing and would still hold people to some degree responsible for their behavior.

We must always hold open the possibility that scientific research in the future may actually succeed in identifying a set of biological conditions for the emergence of homosexual, heterosexual, and transgendered persons. In that new and different situation, we would most certainly be strongly challenged to reconsider and change our current understanding. It would be argued that something that is biologically innate must certainly be natural for a particular person regardless of how unusual it may be.

We need to be prepared for this possible scientific discovery and the arguments that will come from it. The argument, of course, is a morality based on whatever is, is right. But is that true? What it does not take into account is the possibility that what one finds may be part of an abnormal, fallen, disordered world, not part of a normality that God originally created. For example, there is some evidence that some people are genetically predisposed to schizophrenia. If we find some organic cause for schizophrenia, does that mean that is the way they were intended to be? Or is that actually an evidence of the brokenness of the world in which we live?

Even if it were to be proven that there is a biological causation to homosexuality, it would not prove that it is God-given and created. We live after the Fall. Our human nature is fallen, sinful, and abnormal now. 'Normal' in an abnormal world is abnormal. That is the first factor. The second factor is that even if there is a strong tendency, a predisposition from our inheritance, from relationships, from our childhood, etc., the biblical perspective emphasizes our responsibility for our behavior. We are free to make choices. Yes, we are influenced by our genes (in virtually everything we do) and our early family life, but not to the point of complete determinism. Morality is certainly not decided on the basis of genes.

The presence of a strong genetic or psychological predisposition, however, does have a very practical consequence. It should increase the amount of compassion and patience that we exhibit towards those homosexuals for whom the homosexual orientation seems to run deep within their being. We ought to be moved with compassion for the depth of the brokenness experienced. When we talk about this disposition running deep within their being, we are talking about maybe 2% of the population. There are many others who get involved in a gay lifestyle because of a combination of the above-mentioned factors. Others do so because of experimenting with their sexual identity. Still others get involved by choosing homosexuality as an act of rebellion against the majority culture. The homosexual person may not have chosen his orientation, but he has made choices along the way that have been significant in its development and outworking.

In summary, the most credible research on homosexuality to date demonstrates that no one is "born gay." In 1993 a survey by the American Psychiatric Association's Office on International Affairs, established the fact that a majority of psychiatrists internationally view homosexuality as a developmental disorder.[11] Homosexuality is neither innate and unchangeable nor a "life-style choice" and changeable at will. The one with homosexual feelings, desires, and behavior is struggling as a result of a developmental problem. This developmental disorder is most often a deeply embedded condition which normally starts in early childhood long before the development of moral and self-awareness and is genuinely experienced by the individual as though it was never absent in one form or another. It is the result of a varied and mixed combination of genetic factors, gender confusion, family dysfunction, molestation and repeatedly reinforced choices occurring at critical phases of development.

# THREE

## The Gay Lifestyle and Agenda

Before turning to current Christian views on homosexuality, it would be well to look briefly at the lifestyle of
homosexuals. The discussions taking place within the
churches today regarding homosexual orientation and
behavior, the blessing of same-sex unions, and the ordination of practicing homosexuals is not taking place in a
cultural vacuum. It is really a part of larger questions being
asked in society and within Western civilization regarding
sexuality and marriage and the family, albeit taking place
within the arena of the church.

### The Homosexual Lifestyle

What is involved in the homosexual lifestyle that we
are increasingly being asked to accept and see as normal?
Here the gay propagandists are walking a very fine line. On
the one hand they are demanding that the homosexual
lifestyle be accepted as normal. On the other hand they
don't want the general public to know what the lifestyle
really involves. Gay propagandists would like to portray
homosexuals as mature, monogamous, loving individuals who
form and maintain long-lasting, stable relationships in society. And some homosexuals do just that - but very, very few.
The Institute for Sex Research says at most, only 10% of the
homosexual community could be called relatively monogamous. That means that 90% are promiscuous. The homosexual male averages between 20 to106 partners per year,
from 300 to 500 partners in a lifetime, and 27% have had over
1000 sexual partners in a lifetime.[1] Many of these encounters
will be with total strangers in bath houses (nothing to do

with baths), public restrooms and back rooms of gay bars. But what really goes on in homosexual encounters?

I share the following descriptions because I believe that Christians and the general public need to know the fuller picture of what we are facing as a society. Its intent is not to shock and certainly not to offend, nor to arouse disgust or repulsion, but to bring understanding and point out that homosexual practice is *different* in ways that are often harmful, both psychologically and physically. When describing some of the kinds of homosexual physical contact in the second of the two sermons to the congregation, I made sure at the end of the first sermon to tell them that next Sunday's sermon would have some graphic parts to it so parents should use discretion with children. But as their pastor and shepherd I told them that I felt they need to know. The congregation appreciated that advance information. My intent is the same here.

An additional word of caution is needed. It must be kept in mind that there is a variety of homosexual persons. The following profile does not fit those same-sex attracted persons who struggle to live a Godly moral life and are determined to remain chaste. Nor does the profile describe those who are in the process of exiting homosexuality. The profile below is descriptive of sexual behavior for that group of persons who identified themselves as homosexual and who, in one degree or another, are participating in "the lifestyle." While acknowledging the difficulty in arriving at exact figures in such a subject matter, the testimony about homosexual behavior coming from both sides of the debate paints a fairly clear picture of the kinds and frequencies of behavior engaged in by homosexual persons. I shall start with the least disturbing.

First, there is simple physical embrace or touch or kissing. Then there is what is sometimes referred to as "full bodily contact." The two unclothed partners embrace one another and hold each other close, pressing their bodies together. For some men, this in itself is sufficient to produce orgasm with ejaculation.

Then there is mutual masturbation. Each partner stimulates the penis of the other until climax is reached, sometimes successively, sometimes simultaneously. Along with this act may go kissing.

A more intimate sexual contact is *fellatio*. The penis of one man is inserted into the mouth of the other and licking and sucking of the inserted member continues until ejaculation is the result. Fellatio can also be performed mutually and simultaneously, by arranging bodies in such a way that each partner can receive the penis of the other into his mouth. Dr. Stanley Monteith, a medical expert who has studied and researched these kinds of physical contact for over 20 years says that 100% of homosexuals engage in fellatio.[2]

Then there is the act of anal intercourse. This contact involves the insertion of the penis of one of the partners into the anus of the other; the insertion is usually followed by movements of a more or less copulatory nature. Dr. Monteith states that 93% of homosexuals engage in rectal sex. He then goes on to comment that the rectum was not built for intercourse. When that occurs, the rectal mucosa is torn and, in many cases, the sphincter muscles are stretched which can lead to fecal incontinence. It is not a healthy activity because tears in the rectal mucosa result in such a high incidence of disease.

Ninety-two percent of homosexuals engage in something called "rimming". Rimming is simply licking in and around the partner's anus and involves actually placing the tongue into the anus. This action cannot be done without some ingestion of feces.

Then there is something called "fisting". Fisting involves about 47% of homosexuals and involves inserting the fist and arm into a man's rectum so that he would have sexual pleasure and the partner could have pleasure by inflicting this upon him.

Twenty-nine percent of homosexuals engage in something called "golden showers". A man lays on the ground naked and other men stand around and urinate on him. Then there is "scat". About 17% of homosexuals engage in this activity. Scat refers to actively eating human feces or rubbing human feces on the skin or rolling around on the floor in feces, sometimes called 'mud rolling.'

The homosexual acts described by Dr. Monteith are taking place regularly in homosexual lifestyle encounters. We never read or hear about them from gay activists who want us rather to think of loving, caring, monogamous homosexual couples sitting on park benches with their arms around each other. But this is the gay lifestyle homosexualists want society to accept as a perfectly acceptable alternative to the heterosexual relationship. We can perhaps now better understand why there is an epidemic of sexually transmitted diseases in the gay community. No wonder AIDS is such an issue. In 1999, the Medical Institute of Sexual Health reported that, "Homosexual men are at significantly increased risk of HIV/AIDS, hepatitis, anal cancer, gonorrhea and gastrointestinal infections as a result of their sexual practices".[3] Homosexuals have a greater incidence of mental illnesses, particularly depression and suicide, than do heterosexuals. Homosexual behavior clearly endangers men's lives. No wonder the operative word in the gay community is fear.

In spite of homosexual behavior posing serious consequences for the health and well-being of homosexual individuals, leaders in the gay activist movement have organized themselves into one of the most powerful and effective political and public relations campaigns in modern society. They are strong, determined, well-organized, strategic and influential. There is a well thought-out homosexual agenda. The aim of this agenda is to present their lifestyle to the general public as perfectly acceptable.

## The Homosexual Agenda

In a 1989 book entitled *After the Ball* by Harvard graduates and homosexual activists Marshal Kirk and Hunter Madsen, and in a 1987 article titled "The Overhauling of Straight America" by Kirk and Erastes Pill, the authors spell out very clearly the homosexual agenda for America. They list 12 planks in the homosexual platform. I will cite but four of these planks.

1) *Convince everybody in our land that homosexuality is an inborn, involuntary condition.* This propaganda is key

to the homosexual cause. They are bound and determined to convince people that with regard to the homosexual condition and behavior, there is no human choice involved and therefore no value judgments are to be made or received by anyone. They argue that no one makes the choice of being born right-handed or left-handed. So if you are a 'righty' throw the ball with your right hand. If you are a 'lefty' throw the ball with your left hand. Just do what is normal. Go with what you are born with. They infer that since none of us had a choice in being born the way we were born, there are to be no value judgments, there is no morality involved, nothing is right or wrong.

2) *Convince everybody that the sex lives and love lives of homosexuals and heterosexuals are similar and conventional.* There is a concerted effort to portray homosexual persons as being normal and happy individuals and loving, caring, and monogamous couples. The homosexual activists know that the unseemly sides of homosexual behavior have to be suppressed in order to gain acceptance. The masses must not be shocked and repelled by premature exposure to homosexual behavior itself. Sex should be downplayed and gay rights should be reduced to an abstract social question as much as possible. By painting homosexuals' love lives as normal it is believed that people will assume that their sex lives are similar and conventional as well. As Kirk and Pill state: "First let the camel get his nose inside the tent—only later his unsightly derriere!"[4]

The question before us is, in light of the nature of the sexual encounters Dr. Monteith describes, do we consider them conventional? Do we really think homosexual acts fit in commensurately with how God has created our bodies?

3) *Convince everybody that gays and lesbians be given full rights to marry and to adopt children and establish themselves as families.* Gay activists have now lobbied successfully for a change in the marriage laws of Canada. Gay marriage is now legal north of the border. There will be a strong push for America to do the same. In November, 2003, the highest court in Massachusetts ruled that gays had the right to marry under the state constitution. On May

17, 2004, the state of Massachusetts became the first in the nation to legalize homosexual marriages. Gay pressure is being strongly asserted to change adoption laws in this country. In these new "families", young children would grow up in an environment where dads may engage in the kinds of homosexual activity described above. Mothers would be engaged in other kinds of homosexual activity. Gays are working around the clock, and succeeding in some cases, to place gay texts in public schools.

4) *Any resistance to the homosexual agenda be viewed as repugnantly as racism or anti-Semitism.* There is a concerted effort to lump in with bigots and anti-Semites anyone who fails to support the homosexual agenda. If you don't fall in step with the homosexual program you are to be seen as a Nazi. You are to be seen as a social terrorist. You are to be labeled narrow and intolerant. Is it very different in the church? In conjunction with the 38 Primates of the Worldwide Anglican Communion meeting in Lambeth Palace, London, in October, 2003, a retired pro-gay primate at a rally across the Thames River in St. Matthew's Anglican Church, Westminster, referred to those who oppose gay bishops as Taliban zealots.[5]

In these two writings Kirk and Madsen also laid out clearly and unambiguously a six-point strategy to radically change America's perception of homosexual behavior. These six points were:

1.  Talk about gays and gayness as loudly and often as possible.

2.  Portray gays as victims, not aggressive challengers.

3.  Give homosexual protectors a "just" cause.

4.  Make gays look good.

5.  Make the victimizers look bad.

6.  Solicit funds: the buck stops here.

For a more extensive treatment of this six-point strategy, I encourage you to read *The Homosexual Agenda* by Alan Sears and Craig Osten.[6] These authors more fully develop how each point is being played out in present-day American culture. I will but briefly summarize their work here.

*"Talk about Gays and Gayness as Loudly and Often as Possible"*

The premise of this strategic directive is that virtually any behavior begins to look normal if you are exposed to enough of it at close range. History is replete with examples of inhumane and outrageous behaviors becoming commonplace and ordinary. Every modern dictator has understood this principle well. The unthinkable can become the thinkable.

During the 1990s, the onslaught of exposure to homosexual persons was relentless in the media. The number of times we heard about or saw ordinary people who practiced homosexual behavior increased dramatically. Not only has homosexual behavior become commonplace on network television but the homosexual characters are often portrayed as the most compassionate, funny, 'normal' and 'human' persons in the show. This has had the effect of people now seeing homosexual behavior as much more normal than they once did.

The goal of the barrage is to talk about gayness until the issue becomes thoroughly tiresome. The intent is to gradually wear down the public until everyone is so tired of the issue that they throw up their arms and say, "Forget it" and then the homosexual activists get their way.

The next target is organized religion. The strategy here is to neutralize religious authority by first muddying the moral waters. When conservative churches speak against homosexual behavior, then publicize the support more moderate churches give homosexuals. Challenge traditional interpretations of the Bible and expose hatred and inconsistencies. Label conservative churches as homophobic and portray them as antiquated backwaters who are ridiculously out of step with the times and latest findings of psychology and science. Portray any objecting person as poorly informed and uneducated. Portray any advocate as an enlightened, cutting-edge thinker.

*"Portray Gays as Victims, Not Aggressive Challengers"*

This second strategic directive plays directly into most Americans' basic sense of fairness and liberal guilt about anyone who claims to have been oppressed. Homosexual activists have skillfully played the media like a drum to portray homosexuals as a victimized class in need of special protections.

The activists have been ingenious in turning tragic events into opportunities to move their agenda forward. In doing so, they label those who oppose them as 'murderers' or at least sympathizers. We can point here to treatment given the assassination of Harvey Milk, the first openly gay member on the San Francisco Board; the AIDS epidemic of the early 1980's where activists turned a deadly virus health hazard into a civil rights issue; and the brutal and shameless murder of Matthew Shepard by two nonreligious thugs. Following his murder, activists went to the air waves and newsprint and demonized people of faith, laying blame for his murder essentially at the feet of Christians who oppose homosexual behavior.

*"Give Homosexual Protectors a 'Just' Cause"*

This directive feeds into the sensitivities especially of those in society who embrace any group that they are convinced has been 'wronged' in the past. In piggybacking on legitimate efforts to right past wrongs, the activists portray practicing homosexuals as a group in need of protection from a so-called hostile society. Homosexual activists have found in Hollywood a willing ally. Hollywood with its liberal sensitivities and large homosexual community has adopted homosexual behavior as one of its latest causes. Through film and television, Hollywood portrays homosexuals as almost always innocent—the heroes who need protection—while those who oppose them are either boorish or religious fanatics.

*"Make Gays Look Good" and "Make the Victimizers Look Bad"*

The first part of this strategy manifests itself in many ways: from rewriting history to convince people that famous characters were homosexual to the sympathetic portrayal of homosexuals in the media. Regarding the second part, Kirk and Madsen wrote, "We intend to make the antigays look so nasty that the average Americans will want to disassociate themselves from such types."[7] Unfortunately, some Christians have played right into the hands of the gay activists. Fred Phelps and his followers travel the country carrying signs that read "God Hates Fags", picket funerals of AIDS victims and host a website that pictures homosexuals being thrown into hell. Other Christians have been far less loving in discussing the homosexual issue than they ought to be. The gay activists are opportunists and latch on to any such behavior or speech, casting it in the worst possible light and propping it up as representative of bible-believing Christians.

*"Solicit Funds: The Buck Stops Here"*

The strategy here is to get corporate America and major foundations to financially support the homosexual cause. For example, the Gill Foundation has millions in assets and provides grants to promote the homosexual agenda through its subsidiary, the Gay and Lesbian Fund for Colorado, to groups such as the Easter Seals, the American Lung Association, the Urban League and the Girl Scouts. There are strings attached to the money, however. Each organization that accepts grants from the Foundation must agree to add homosexual behavior to its antidiscrimination policies and publicly credit the fund in its material.

The Gill Foundation has given large sums of money to groups like the Lambda Legal Defense and Education Fund. Both of these organizations lobby for same-sex marriage. The Lambda Legal Defense has been the leader in the attack against the Boy Scouts for its policy regarding homosexual scoutmasters and boasts corporate support from IBM and United Airlines. The Human Rights Campaign lobbies for and supports political candidates sympathetic to the homosexual agenda and lists American Airlines and Subaru as corporate sponsors. The gay activists have been very successful in getting corporate America to support the homosexual cause.

The vision of the homosexual agenda is clear. It has concrete planks. It knows what it believes and where it wants to go. It has goals and objectives. It also has a clear strategy on how to get there. Listen to a brief excerpt from the final pages of *After the Ball* as it describes the future of the gay agenda: "We know exactly what we want...and will do whatever must be done to secure it."[8] One page later, the authors discuss what is going to motivate or drive their movement. They ask the questions rhetorically,

"And where, for that matter, is the steam supposed to come from? Your patriotism and sense of fair play? Your homophile zeal? Benevolent love of your gay brothers and sisters? Agape?

"No . . . America in the 1990s is the time and place for rage—ice cold, controlled, directed rage. Tomorrow, the real gay revolution begins."[9]

The 90s are now behind us. We are now in the tomorrow. It's a new day.

**Part 2**

# Is Homosexuality Contrary to the Will of God?

# FOUR

# Four Christian Views

Within the 21$^{st}$ Century Christian church in the West, there are different views of homosexuality. Since the 1950s there has been a growing division of opinion among Christians. As I am able to discern, there currently are four main views within the major Protestant denominations. Sadly, the major denominations are seriously divided on this issue. Since the late '70s and the '80s, they have spent many weary hours in their sessions, synods, dioceses, and special conferences studying, reporting, discussing and debating the issue. It is disturbing that there appears to be so little agreement.

1. The first view is that homosexuality is the **worst of sins**. This is the view that was particularly prevalent during the medieval period. It is still to be found in the church today. People with this rather Greek view of sin have said that anyone who struggles with homosexual feelings, thoughts and behavior is wicked. The Greek view of reality is that the things of the soul and spirit are high and all important and the things of the body and material world are low and unimportant. Homosexual sin, then, is seen as worse than other sins. It is seen as especially horrific and evil.

2. A second view is that homosexuality is the **lesser of two evils.** This view says that we live in a non-ideal situation. Therefore, committed homosexual relationships are not necessarily good, but they are better than seeking physical release by picking up partners for a 'one-night stand' or by the use of prostitutes. A loving relationship is

better than to sublimate or in some other way deal with your temptation to sin. It is better to be in a loving, committed, homosexual relationship than to burn with passion.

H. Kimball Jones is one who would be representative of this view. In an article entitled "Towards a Christian Understanding of the Homosexual" Jones states, "The Church must be willing to make the difficult, but necessary step of recognizing the validity of mature homosexual relationships, encouraging the absolute invert to maintain a fidelity to one partner when his only other choice would be to lead a promiscuous life filled with guilt and fear. This would by no means be an endorsement of homosexuality by the Church."[1]

By 'invert' Kimball means the person who has a strong homosexual orientation. Notice the assertion that the invert's only other choice is a promiscuous life. The underlying assumption is that the homosexual person is who he is and he cannot be anything else. This view would say that the Bible has been misinterpreted, that in fact the Bible does not condemn homosexuality in a loving, caring situation. It is the lesser of two evils.

3. The third view is that the **Bible is not relevant to our contemporary social situation.** This view holds that it is clear that homosexual practices are condemned in Scripture, but because these acts are part of idolatrous cults and temple prostitution or part of the Jewish ritual code, these condemnations ought not be carried over into the Gentile world and into our world today. The contention is that in Romans 1 Paul is condemning promiscuous homosexual acts by *heterosexual* persons, not sexual acts by people with strong homosexual orientations. These heterosexual persons are acting against their heterosexual nature and therefore should not do it. These people are not persons who have a homosexual orientation and who are acting against a divinely intended heterosexual norm or pattern in nature. The Bible is speaking to an entirely different cultural and historic setting, it is argued, and what it says simply does not address the matter of caring and committed same-sex relationships. It is not relevant to the current situation.

This view in particular is tied to the publication in 1955 of Sherwin Bailey's book, *Homosexuality & The Western Christian Tradition*. This writing was the first serious challenge to the Bible's condemnation of homosexuality. In his book Bailey, an Anglican theologian, argues for the acceptance of homosexuality. This was a watershed publication for the Gay Christian Movement who uses it as their biblical commentary. Their conviction is that homosexuality is a gift of God to be gladly accepted, enjoyed and honored, but within the context of loving relationships. They believe it is compatible with the Christian faith not only to love a person of the same sex, but also to express that love fully in a physical sexual relationship.

This third view is saying, then, that rather than striving by hook or by crook to obtain a Bible which doesn't condemn homosexuality, let's be honest and freely accept the fact that we have a Bible that does condemn homosexuality. Let it be further understood, it is allegedly argued, that this Bible also reflects belief in other things that we no longer accept today, such as the flat earth, slavery or the subordination of women. Let us accept it but then understand that it is not relevant to us in our present cultural situation and the Biblical judgments against homosexuality are not relevant to today's debate.

Robin Scroggs in *The New Testament and Homosexuality* would be representative of this third view. He states concisely and straightforwardly that,

> "Biblical judgments against homosexuality are not relevant to today's debate. They should no longer be used in denominational discussions about homosexuality. . . . (I) argue that the Scriptures are irrelevant and provide no help in the heated debate today . . . Once the Biblical injunctions are eliminated from discussion, once the Bible ceases to be used as a bludgeon for whatever side, then all of us are thrown into a situation where none of us are knowers. . . ."[2]

The Bible's teaching, it is argued, is bound to a particular cultural and religious background and cannot be applied directly to our modern day situation. Proponents of this view would claim to accept the authority of the Bible and yet would reject much of its teaching as being outdated and irrelevant.

Some proponents of this view take it a step further. They say that the Bible is not only irrelevant on the homosexual issue, but that it is simply wrong. Walter Wink, in his book *Homosexuality and the Christian Faith* writes:

> "Where the Bible mentions homosexual behavior at all, it clearly condemns it. I freely admit that. The issue is precisely whether the biblical judgment is correct. . . If now new evidence is in on the phenomenon of homosexuality, are we not obligated—no, free—to reevaluate the whole issue in light of all the available data and decide what is right under God, for ourselves?"[3]

Peter Gomes, a homosexual pastor at Harvard University, argues in his book, *The Good Book: Reading the Bible with Mind and Heart,* that the Christian Church has arrived at a more enlightened position than what the Bible says about slavery and women. Therefore, he says, we should do the same with respect to homosexuality. I will be addressing the matters of slavery and women in ministry in a later chapter.

4. The fourth view is that the **Bible is relevant to our contemporary social situation.** This view holds that the homosexual condition is a result of being part of a broken, fallen world. It is the *practice* of homosexuality rather than orientation which is contrary to the will of God. Proponents would see homosexual orientation as being contrary to the will of God in the sense of being the result of the brokenness and fallenness of humankind. Those holding to this view would accept the full authority of the Bible believing its teachings are extremely relevant to the current issue of homosexuality today.

This is the view held by nearly all Christian theologians until about 50 years ago. They condemned homosexual behavior as wrong. They saw it as part of the disorder and brokenness of the fallen world and a deviation from the divine intention of creation. Tertullian, Augustine, Aquinas all spoke of homosexual behavior as being against nature.

The Reformers, Martin Luther and John Calvin, were strongly against same-sex behavior but stressed that it is no more or less serious than fornication, adultery, and other expressions of sin. This view is based primarily on the creation ordinance of a man leaving his father and mother and cleaving to his wife and the two becoming one flesh. (Genesis 2:24) This ordinance is then believed to be supported by other Scriptures that condemn homosexual practice.

This fourth view holds that the relevance of the Bible's teaching is that we all have a sinful nature inherited from the sin of Adam and Eve and further shaped through the sins of others who have affected us and twisted us and bent us. But it is the *practice* of homosexuality that is sinful. The thoughts of homosexual temptation that I have and the desires that accompany them may arise from my bent, broken, sinful nature and a mixture of genetic, intrauterine or postnatal factors, just as if I might have thoughts of losing my temper, of pride, of arrogance or of incredible fear or anxiety rising up within me. I haven't chosen these thoughts or feelings or desires. But I am responsible for what I *do* with them and how I react to them. So it is the outworking of thoughts and desires that is sinful, whether that outworking is playing with fantasies and allowing temptation to grow in my mind or actually acting on it in a homosexual lifestyle.

Many who hold this fourth view prefer not to talk about 'homosexual people' as such. They believe that designation tends to define persons by only one small, particular aspect of their identity. Rather, they prefer to talk about persons with homosexual thoughts and feelings and desires just as they talk about people who struggle with anger and pride and covetousness.

One can see why there is so much confusion among Christians as they are surrounded and confronted by these various streams of thought within the Church today.

# FIVE

## The Great Divide—Biblical Authority

When discussing the phenomenon of homosexuality, at some point someone undoubtedly will make an appeal to the Scriptures. They will say, "Such and such a text says this about homosexual behavior". But as soon as Scripture is brought into the conversation something inevitably happens. Whether in formal debate or one-on-one casual conversation, the moment comes when someone cries out, *"But, it all depends on your interpretation!"* The debate quickly turns from there into a quotation contest centered narrowly on a handful of texts in which everything is reduced to the pitting of one interpretation against another. Each person has an expert theologian or author they quote who can trump the expert theologian or author that the other person quotes.

After the debate has become exhausted at the level of quoting Scripture, it turns to the relating of Scripture to the data gathered from science and experience. But when it turns in this direction, we are again hopelessly back in a low-land fog in which one interpretation can always look as good as another. This scientific study is more valid than that scientific study. This person's experience counters that person's experience. We sink into the quicksand of opinion and interpretation that loses sight of the particularity of the claims at issue which cannot cope with the passion and tenacity with which these opinions and interpretations are argued and held. We are stuck in a bog of never ending opinions and counter opinions, of interpretations and counter interpretations. It is a stalemate that ends up trivializing the debate.

What is often not seen or acknowledged is that there is something much deeper here than merely some scientific report or human experience or simple application of some ancient text. There is something far more crucial here than the pitting of opinions and interpretations one against the other. What is not perceived is that the appeal to the biblical-historical understanding of Scripture is essentially an appeal to revelation. It is an appeal to God's Word to us. In the current debate on homosexuality, the crucial question is, "Do we have a Word from God? Has God communicated His will to us regarding human sexuality and homosexual behavior?" If in fact God has not spoken into the world and told us what is right and what is wrong, there is no solid basis for any moral distinctions, nor is there any knowledge of what those moral distinctions are. If he has not spoken, we are left only with finite human opinions and we are in no position to say that one is better than another.

Let me try to clarify the importance of this appeal to the biblical-historical understanding of Scripture as revelation. Through our reason and experience we can know a great deal about ourselves and the world in which we live. We have wonderful cognitive powers that give us much knowledge. We experience the wonders of the world in which we live. We experience ourselves as human beings living in this world. Yet, without undermining their importance, we also must say that human experience and reason give us only partial knowledge of who we are and the world around us. Therefore, in and of themselves, reason and experience are insufficient and inadequate. The history of philosophy clearly has shown this insufficiency to be true and our own experiences bear witness as well. The Christian depends finally on God's revelation to tell us who we are, how we are to live, and the nature and shape of the world around us. It is only through divine revelation, then, that we can know our true nature as God intended it to be.

When one travels east and west across the western half of the United States on Interstate 80, at an elevation of 7000 feet in the Colorado Mountains between Rawlins and Rock Springs, Wyoming, one crosses a great watershed. It is imperceptible to the human eye. Outwardly, during the winter months, the snow lies there in a seemingly unbroken unity. However, the unity is an illusion, for it lies along a great divide, the Continental Divide. When the snow melts, one portion of the snow flows westward making its way through valleys and streams and rivers and finally to the Pacific Ocean. The portion of the snow that lies close beside meanders its way eastward and southward through valleys and streams and rivers toward the Gulf of Mexico. Once water begins flowing in each direction, it ends up literally a thousand miles apart. We know where it will finally end up.

The great divide in the homosexual debate is the authority of Scripture.

The essential understanding of the Scriptures on the one side of the divide is that they were written by humans who were using their own experiences to try to understand God's ways.

In this view the authority of the Bible comes essentially from man's initiative. On this side of the divide, authority is tied to the latest discoveries and hypotheses of science, as contemplated by learned professors. On this side the vicissitudes of human experience are drawn upon heavily to give insight and meanings. Reason and experience are the ultimate authority in the interpretation of the ancient biblical texts. This view sees the human interpretation of the text as the final authoritative word.

The understanding of the Scriptures on the other side of the divide is that the words of the Bible are essentially the effort of God to help us understand our experiences.

In this view the authority of the Bible comes from God's initiative. Scripture is understood as God's revelation to us. It is God's Word to us. The ultimate authority for faith is tied to the Scriptures. This is where Martin Luther and the Protestant Reformation tied their faith to authority in the battles of their day.

It is fashionable today for those on the first side of the Divide to belittle and verbally assail those on the second side. Such reliance on the Bible as God's peculiar revelation is unthinkable from this side of the Divide. So straw men are constructed and then ridiculed. The charge is made that the people on the other side of the Divide are 'literalists' who take the literal meaning of any and every word in the Bible. But it is a hollow charge. The truth is there are no such literalists. They don't exist. I have never run across anyone anywhere who believes literally that the mountains clapped their hands. I don't know of anyone who thinks that King Herod ran around on four legs with a bushy tail, even though Jesus called him, "that fox." Yet the charge is made that these people believe the Bible in this way.

The charge is further made that those who believe that God's Word is spoken in the words of the Bible are bibliolaters. The accusation is that they are guilty of worshiping the Bible for they actually put their trust in the Bible itself! Our trust is to be in God, they ridicule, not in pages of paper. This claim also has no substance. I know of no one who worships the pages of a book. It is a straw man. These accusations of literalism and bibliolatry against those who place their faith in the Bible as God's revelation need to be exposed for what they are—false and without foundation. These claims should not go unchallenged.

In what way then shall we understand the Bible as God's revelation to us? George Muedeking in a paper titled "Christ's Scripture or Scripture's Christ—Is It an Either-Or?" gives us an extremely helpful exercise in helping us understand the relationships between God, Scripture, and faith.[1] Muedeking says, "Imagine receiving a telephone message at work that says, 'David, your house is on fire. Better get home quick'"! What do you do?

In order to believe any message like this one given over the phone, first, you must quickly determine if the *messenger* is trustworthy. If the messenger is known to be a liar, a prankster, or capricious, you will most likely have good reasons to disregard the message. If he is trustworthy, however, you will undoubtedly act on the message. The messenger who speaks the message in the Bible is Jesus Christ Himself. It is Jesus who "authenticates" the words of the Bible. We trust them because we trust the messenger. He is the Authority for the authority of the Bible over us.

Secondly, and quite separately, in order to believe "your house is on fire", you must certainly also believe the *message* itself, that the words themselves are valid. It is possible to believe in the trustworthiness of the messenger and yet not believe in the message he brings. While fully believing in the messenger, I may think that what he is telling me so urgently is not to be believed: the house he is talking about has to be the one next door; he has been dreaming and just woke up thinking it was really happening; he may be pulling an "April Fool" joke on me!

For me to act on the message and go home quickly, I must have confidence in both the message and the messenger at the same time. In the same way, for me to have eternal life and to live the new life there is in Christ, I must believe both in the words of the Bible and the Christ who so graciously offers them to me.

Martin Luther spoke of the Scriptures as the manger in which Christ lies. In light of Luther's theology of the Word, this analogy would mean that we are to believe both in the manger and in the Christ Child. Without the manger we have no knowledge of the Christ. Without Christ we have no manger. I must believe in both the messenger and the message he brings.

In our day, Luther's picture of the manger and Christ child has been divorced from his understanding of God's Word and manipulated to make Luther say something different. It is argued that Christians do not worship the manger (the Bible), rather they worship the Christ whom the manger contains. It is argued that we are to have confidence in the God of the Bible, not in the words of the Bible themselves. So Luther's writings are meticulously screened to find any statements that might hint of any distrust of the Scripture's words in favor of his having found his faith from his relationship with Christ himself. The search has been unsuccessful, however, because of Luther's frequently expressed personal gratitude for the revelation that the Scriptures alone gave him about how a person comes into a right relationship with God.

We do not 'believe in the Bible' in exactly the same way that we do not 'believe in the telephone' that conveyed the message that told me my house was burning down. Rather, we believe in BOTH the message AND the messenger. We speak of the Bible, then, as a means of grace. The Bible is the means, the instrument, the telephone—if you will—that God uses to speak His words to us. God is a personal God who has created us in his image. A distinctive part of that image of God is our ability to communicate in language like our Creator. It is therefore perfectly fitting that God has communicated to us in the same way as He has created us to communicate with each other. The words of the Bible are the means the messenger has chosen to communicate his message to us. That is why God is the Authority for the authority of the Bible over us. Both the messenger and the message are the object of our faith at the same time. Both must be present in our hearts if we are to live responsibly as Christian believers.

So again, we need to comprehend that the authority of Scripture is the Continental Divide in the homosexual debate. We are either dealing with a view of biblical authority that sees the human interpretation of the text as the final word—and with the setting up of this alternative authority the Scriptures can be made finally to say something quite different than their normal and simple meaning—or with a view that sees Scripture as God's revelation to us whose authority rests within itself because it is given by God. Either there is or there is not a revelation from God.

Now to be sure, when one receives Scripture as God's revelation, one has to interpret (understand) a revelation. It is also true that one has to think through the application of divine revelation in new cultural and historical settings. These require the full mustering of the best of our cognitive powers. As such, interpretations of an uncertain text may legitimately differ. There may be differences of interpretation on the same side of the Divide. There may be agreement in interpretations across the Divide. There may be inconsistencies on both sides. But there is all the difference in the world in what is at stake once the issue is cast properly in terms of revelation. Our understandings may be incomplete but the revelation from God still comes to us. One is no longer simply wrestling with a book or a set of purely human texts. One is wrestling with the will of God.

And once one yields to God's will, the call upon that life is to obey it, live according to it, and be prepared to die for it if necessary. We are no longer living in the comfortable and cozy world of academia. We are dealing with the Word of God.

Before moving on to consider the biblical material, I think it important here at the beginning to tell you which of the four Christian views I find myself holding and on which side of the Continental Divide regarding the authority of Scripture I stand. I do so because I will be approaching the following Scripture discussions from these viewpoints. It is only fair and honest that I tell you before beginning.

I number myself among those who hold to the historical-biblical understanding of Scripture as God's propositional revelation to us and I believe that its teachings are extremely relevant to the current issue of homosexuality. Because I stand in this place, the crucial texts in the discussion are not confined to a few passages in the Old and New Testaments that condemn homosexual acts. For sure, these have their place in the debate on human sexuality. Indeed, seeing God's intention for all of life across the span of the two testaments is one of the tasks of moral theology. However, the central passages become those that represent the teaching of Jesus Christ on marriage.

When one appeals to Scripture as revelation, our Lord's teaching can no longer simply be added in as one more item in a list of texts. Jesus' words become the central authoritative teaching and all other passages are to be seen in light of this center. That is why before turning to the biblical passages that speak of homosexual acts, we will turn to Jesus' affirmation of the creation accounts of Genesis and the divine intention for marriage. But first a look at the task of biblical interpretation.

# SIX

## Interpreting the Bible

Before we look at the biblical texts themselves, it is critical to think about how we approach the interpretation of Scripture with regard to the passages that deal with marriage and homosexual acts. There are two theological words that come into play here whose meanings we need to know. *Exegesis* literally means "leading out". The task of exegesis is to expound or explain the meaning of the Bible, to "lead out" of the text its meaning. Exegesis deals with what the Bible actually teaches about homosexuality. *Hermeneutics* means the science of interpretation. The task of hermeneutics is to discern how that teaching should be interpreted. Hermeneutics involves moving from what the text 'meant' in its cultural milieu to what the text 'means' for our own day. Then *ethics* deals with the task of how the bible's teachings should be applied today. The task of understanding the Bible, then, involves both exegesis and hermeneutics, both ascertaining the original meaning of the text and then discerning how that text is to be applied to us today.

If the Bible is what it claims to be, the Word of God, and if in the Scriptures we have God's written communication to man, then we are meant to understand it.

The key to the whole idea of hermeneutics, it seems to me, is found in two central truths of the Bible. First, the Bible tells us that God is a Person. Secondly, the Bible tells us that we are persons made in the image of God.

Secular scientists today note that what distinguishes Man from non-man is that Man is the verbal communicator. If language, then, is one of the basic links between human beings and God, we would expect that when God communicates to Man, He does so through the ordinary use of language.

God intends for us to understand his message to us. We treat the Bible, then, as we treat any piece of literature. We read it to understand what the writer is saying. We do not approach the Bible as a magical or mystical or hidden book full of tricky, obscure, and esoteric things. Rather, through the means of this book, God communicates to human beings through the ordinary use of language. Basically, we read the Bible no differently than we read the daily newspaper.

So the task in approaching the Bible is the same task as approaching any written communication. What we are attempting to do is to ascertain the intended meaning of the author. We come to the writing with the question, "What is the author seeking to communicate to us? What is the innate meaning of the text"?

Some people at this place have used the term "literal interpretation" to describe their approach to the Bible. If one uses these words, he or she needs to be aware of two inherent problems with this phrase. The first problem is the word "literal!" The second problem is the word "interpretation!" When someone uses this phrase they need to be prepared to explain what they mean by it. The reason is that the word 'literal' today has become a trick word. If someone asks you, "Do you take the Bible literally?" and you say "yes" they immediately open up the Bible to passages like, *The mountains skipped like rams!* or *Let the hills sing for joy!* and you look foolish. If you say you don't take the Bible literally you are asked then how do you take it. Perhaps a better word would be the word 'straightforward.' We take the Bible straightforwardly, understanding the words and phrases of Scripture within the literary genre in which they are written.

What those who use the phrase "literal interpretation" mean is that they take the language of the Bible in its simple, ordinary and straightforward sense. There is no trickery involved. They interpret the Bible according to the simple and common meanings of the words and the normal rules of grammar. It is the method of interpretation commended by Martin Luther when he wrote,

> "No violence is to be done to the words of God, whether by man or angel; but [the Scriptures] are to be retained in their simplest meaning wherever possible, and to be understood in their grammatical and literal sense unless the context plainly forbids."[1]

One needs to explain, however, that while we take the Bible in its literal sense, not everything in the Bible is to be read literalistically. Because not all language is literal! We recognize different literary forms—poetry, parables, didactic portions, historical narrative. We do not read the Bible without regard to the ordinary rules of literature. There are different types of literature and different idioms of speech. When you tell your wife that you "bumped into Nancy at the mall today," you don't mean (or usually you don't mean!) you actually had physical contact with Nancy. You just mean you met her in the mall. Similarly, we talk about the sun rising in the east and setting in the west. We are not talking literally here. Language is full of these kinds of idioms. We have only to listen to our own speech during a normal day to realize how much of our language is not literal in the precise sense.

The word "interpretation" also can be problematic. It is problematic when it gives the impression that the Bible has no definite meaning of its own, as though it is some sort of molten metal that has no shape until you give it shape. Someone says, "It all depends on your interpretation". That is not at all what we mean when we use the word. The Bible has an intrinsic meaning. There is an innate meaning in the text. The author is trying to communicate something to us. Our task is not to interpret the Bible. The Bible, in fact, interprets us. Our task is to understand the Bible. 'Understand' is then perhaps the better word to use today.

The task of understanding the Bible is not a complicated thing. When we read the morning newspaper, we do so with the expectation of opening it up, of letting it speak to us, of understanding it. When we open the Bible to read it, we can have the same expectation. It is far less complicated than is often suggested. We must never allow ourselves to be maneuvered into seeing the Bible as an impenetrable jungle with snakes and scorpions all over the place. This dread comes over you as you picture yourself hacking your way through a jungle in South America. It is not something terribly complicated like that. There is a clear road before us that we can walk down.

This does not mean, however, that all detailed exegesis is therefore simple. Nor does it mean that there are no problems in ascertaining what a word or phrase or passage means. As we walk down the road of interpretation (understanding) there are difficulties. Sometimes the mist sets in. Sometimes a tree is fallen across the path. There are difficulties, but the interpretive task is not the picture of an impenetrable jungle that we must hack our way through.

The Bible is no different from our morning newspaper when it comes to understanding it. But then why is it that the Bible *is* so much more difficult to understand than our daily newspaper? Let me deal here with two major problems, two huge trees that lie across the road of interpretation making the way difficult.[2]

When I pick up the Minneapolis Tribune, I understand that this newspaper in my hands is a product of its own environment. In Wales, where I am writing this, I understand that *The Guardian* newspaper I read each day is a product of a British environment. I likewise understand when I open up and read the Bible that the Bible is not a product of either an American or British environment in terms of its language, culture, history or geography. I understand that the Bible comes out of a different world, the world of the ancient near East. There is a gap between my world and the biblical world in terms of language, culture, and geography.

**The first major difficulty to understanding the Bible is the problem of bridging the gap**. Our task is to bridge this gap by putting ourselves in the shoes of those to whom the various parts of the Bible were written. God did not communicate His message abstractly. He communicated His message in a particular historical and cultural setting.

Despite this gap, it is not that I read the Bible and cannot understand anything. There is a great deal that I can read straightforwardly and understand. But until I can put myself within the setting of the Bible, my understanding is going to be limited. As I understand more and more of the language, culture, history and geography, I get greater and greater insight into the meaning. There is no easy solution to bridging the gap. The only way to overcome the gap and to put yourself in the shoes of those to whom the Bible was given is good, hard study and/or sitting under the tutelage of someone who can teach you.

Recently, two women in the congregation I serve have been befriending a woman from Japan. In a work situation the first of these two friends has shared her faith in Jesus Christ with this Japanese woman and witnessed to her the reality of a resurrected and living Christ who loves people so much he died for them. Over time this woman, who has a Buddhist background, has been drawn to investigate Christianity more closely because of the love and care and lifestyle of this Christian friend. She was given a Japanese Bible and began to read it. The two women spent hours upon hours discussing the meaning of words and passages and concepts where the one would ask the other questions about the meaning of the Bible stories. The friend would struggle to find words and phrases and illustrations that would convey Christian concepts to a Buddhist mindset.

In time, the second Christian friend also began meeting regularly with this woman for specific Bible study. They would read passages together and, in a tutor role, this second friend would try to explain and interpret the meaning of passages to her. Both these friends were helping to bridge the gap of language, culture and history between two totally different worlds for their Japanese friend. In that long process the woman was able gradually to put herself in the shoes of those to whom the Bible was written, to understand the love of God in Christ for her, and happily has come to trust Christ as Savior. It can be a difficult road, but the gap can be bridged.

**The second major difficulty—the problem of removing our glasses—is much more serious and crucial.**

We may have been successful in moving past the first fallen tree on our road of interpretation only to immediately be faced with a second. The distance of the cultural and historical gap has been overcome sufficiently, but now as I come to the Bible, I am confronted by the message itself. I suddenly become profoundly involved. I am drawn into the message and thereby lose objectivity. I am confronted with all the basic issues of human existence: "Does God exist?" "Who is man?" "Are there moral absolutes?" "Am I guilty?" The message of the Bible confronts me personally. It speaks to who I am. When I am so confronted by the Bible's message, I am no longer able to be neutral or detached.

At this point of confrontation, two things meet. The message of the Bible confronts me. And I confront the message with all my preconceived notions, pet theories, biases, prejudices and presuppositions. We immediately tend to read the Bible through our own preconceived notions. As such, we look for what we think ought to be there. Or we look for what we want to find there. We are not really open to what really is there.

The following illustration might help us to see what is involved here more clearly. Let's suppose that five relatively intelligent men are identified who are absolutely naïve about the Bible. None of them have ever heard of the Bible before. They have no preconceived notions about it, no vested interest in it, no biases regarding it. Nothing. You approach these five men and say to them, "Here is a book called the Bible. I will pay each of you $500 and want you to go away for a month and read it from beginning to end. At the end of the month, I want you to come back and tell me what the book says". I am quite sure that when those five men came back, they would give substantially the same report as to what the book says.

Then you take five different men and ask them to do exactly the same thing. These five men are as follows: an arch fundamentalist preacher from the Deep South; a liberal theologian just graduated from Harvard Divinity School; a Hindu mystic fresh from living 20 years in an ashram in northern India; a mature, sophisticated Jewish rabbi from New York City; and a hard-core atheist. You approach these five men and say to them, "I've got a book here called the Bible. I want you each to read it and report back what the book says". My guess is that you wouldn't be able to tell from their reports that they had read the same book!

The Bible essentially is a clean and simple book. But because the Bible strikes so close to home and raises such basic human issues, we cannot be objective toward it. We read it through the glasses of our preconceived ideas. Therefore, as we come to the Bible, what we must do is remove our glasses. That is the most difficult of things to do. But however difficult, we must make the conscious attempt not to impose our own ideas, our own framework upon the Bible. We must let the Bible speak for itself and listen to it with openness. We must make an effort to hear what the Bible is saying. This is as true for Christians as for non-Christians. No one is neutral or unbiased here. All of us are heavily indoctrinated. It will be a struggle to set aside the glasses. But every time we come to the Bible, we need to make a conscious effort not to sift it through our own grid. We need to remove our glasses.

Now it must be acknowledged that it is impossible to totally separate one's self from one's own period of history with its particular concerns. These concerns will inevitably affect us as we come to read the Bible. We can think, for example, of the 16th Century Reformers, Luther and Calvin, and the problem they faced in this area of removing their glasses. They grew up with the concept of Christendom deeply embedded within them. In their world the entire community was Christian. That reality couldn't help but affect them when they came to read the Bible.

The Reformers were brought up inside the Roman Catholic Church, some of them in monasteries. But they were able to shed their cultural and intellectual trappings to such a degree that they allowed the Bible to speak for itself once again. Central teachings of the Bible were once again allowed to emerge from its pages.

As the Reformers did, so we must do. We have to identify and then firmly lay aside these other ideas in order to let the Bible speak for itself with its own message.

Objective study, then, as though there is no subjective element is impossible. We can never totally divest ourselves from our times and culture. But what I am saying is we are to realize the difficulties and attempt resolutely to identify and stand away from other ideas in our culture that we have inherited from different world views.

Let me further illustrate a few of these worldviews that have confronted the Church and caused such problems. We think of the enormous influence of Platonism in the early Church through Alexandria and Origin. When the Church interpreted through its dualistic Greek lens what the New Testament meant by Paul's term 'the flesh,' it led to the exaltation of male celibacy, the restriction of sex in marriage to procreation, and reinforced the inferior status of women.

Or, we think of the dominance of Aristotelianism in the Church of the 14th and 15th Centuries - illustrated well by Thomas Aquinas' teaching that "once having produced the maximal or optimal number of children, a parent cannot have non-generative intercourse without sin unless a refusal to do his or her conjugal duty might drive the other partner to commit adultery".[3]

The worldviews of these philosophers deeply influenced the Church's understanding when reading the Bible. By setting up the dictatorships of Plato and Aristotle, the Church had set bounds to the intellect more effectively than she had ever been able to do by means of dogma. The Bible was read through the lenses of these alternative philosophies and, consequently, the Bible was made to say something that it does not say.

In our recent history, it has been the same with the lens of naturalism, the philosophy that there is no supernature and there are no miracles. There is the lens of evolution and how this whole philosophy has affected our thinking about the world and the Bible. There is the lens of existentialism in the Church in what is called neo-orthodoxy. Process theology is a lens, a worldview that leaves everything finally open ended. Many today read the Bible through the lens of liberation thought. Like Platonism and Aristotelianism before them, these alternative worldviews also are dictators that have bound the intellects of men and women, alternative philosophies through whose lenses the Bible has been read. Reading the Bible through these glasses does not allow the Bible to speak for itself but in fact construes the Bible to say something it does not say.

But it is not just the learned scholars who are challenged to remove their glasses. It is all of us. I think of the woman who has lived in a horribly abusive marriage. Her husband is a selfish autocrat who verbally and physically abused her for years. It was always his way or the highway. She finally gets out of the marriage. This woman then reads where the Bible says, *"Wives, be subject to your husbands as you are to the Lord."* Do you think that maybe her experience of years of abuse might tempt her to read the Apostle Paul's words through the lens of pain and anger? She will most probably be tempted to read them through a hermeneutic of pain. A probable result may be that either she will think that Paul means something far different than what his words appear to say or she will simply disregard Paul as a woman-hater and his teachings on men, women and marriage as hopelessly outdated. In this case the abusive personal experience has become the 'alternative philosophy,' the lens that does not allow Paul to speak for himself.

Or again, think of a young man who has always felt himself to be different. He discovers that he is gay. He never remembers physical feelings for girls, only feelings and desires for boys. He didn't choose to be this way. It is just the way he is. He surmises that he was born this way. He finds satisfaction and fulfillment in a homosexual relationship where his love for his partner is expressed physically. This man then reads where the Bible says, *"You shall not lie with a male as with a woman; it is an abomination."*

Do you think that maybe his life-long experience of homosexual thoughts, feelings, desires and finally behavior may affect how he reads these words from Leviticus? He may well be tempted to read them through his own life's homosexual experience. He may search for, find and agree with a theologian who holds to the position that the Levitical passage is not speaking to loving, committed same-sex relationships. In this case, one's particular sexual experience has become the lens that does not let the biblical text speak for itself. Removing our glasses as we approach Scripture can be extremely difficult but crucially necessary in the task of ascertaining the native meaning of the Bible.

These two major problems make the Bible hard to understand. It takes effort to remove these two huge trees that lie across the road of interpretation. But they are not insurmountable. We can move past them and come to greater and greater understanding of the intended meaning of the biblical writers.

## Additional Principles of Interpretation

In addition to overcoming these two major difficulties, there are some additional principles on the road of interpretation that will help us in coming to an understanding of the Bible and its message. The following four would be among them:

1) *Consult the author.* This is the surest way of ascertaining meaning. If you read an article in the morning paper and are confused by what it says, the best course of action would be to call up the local news department and ask the author for an explanation. With the Bible, happily, calling upon the Author is also possible. God is the ultimate Author of the books of the Bible, and the same Holy Spirit who guided the human writers in their writing has also been given to the readers. With the Psalmist we can ask, *"Open my eyes, so that I may behold wondrous things out of your law"*. We can ask the God who communicated to us through his human writers for an understanding of that communication.

There would be two warnings here. First, the Holy Spirit does not communicate to us any doctrine not already contained in Scripture. The Holy Spirit makes us wise up to what is written—not beyond. The Psalmist asked that God would open his eyes to understand what is *already there*. When the Church sets the Word against the Spirit, at that point it borders on becoming cultic. The Word is nullified from judging claims to new revelation. We become enthusiasts and subjectivists and move into the same place of Jehovah's Witnesses and Mormons who claim new revelations which go beyond Scripture. There is no new revelation beyond Scripture.

Second, inspiration is infallible, but illumination is not. Inspiration is the Holy Spirit, without in any way abrogating the humanness and personalities of the authors, moving the human writers along in their writing of Scripture. Illumination is the process by which the Holy Spirit guides the human readers in their understanding. Illumination is not infallible. God has chosen to give us a God-breathed, wholly accurate book but not inerrant understanding. Even though we pray for God to give us understanding, it does not mean that our understanding is infallible. We have no such guarantee.

2) *Use Biblical helps.* You are not the first person who has read the Bible under the guidance of the Holy Spirit. The Holy Spirit has guided Godly men and women in the past who have consecrated their entire lives to the study of Scripture. It would not be the better part of wisdom to ignore their labors. Learn from people who have lived before you who have written down their insights.

There are many biblical helps available. An accurate Bible translation that is reliable and readable is most important. This is the first place where Godly people will help you in your understanding. A good concordance takes every word in the Bible and tells you where it can be found so you can see how a word is used and discern its meaning. A commentary will give you a verse by verse explanation of the Bible. Now just because a commentary says something doesn't necessarily mean it is true, but a good commentary is of great help. A Bible dictionary gives you short articles on names, places and theological ideas. All these can be of great assistance in reading the Bible to understand it.

Just a word of caution regarding biblical helps. These helps are good guides but poor masters. Remember that they are written by fallible humans. We are not bound by these helps. Therefore, use them only insofar as they shed light on the Scriptures. We have no pope. In the last analysis, we each are responsible for understanding the Bible for ourselves.

3) *Let Scripture interpret Scripture.* The Bible is its own best commentary. The Bible is not some religious anthology. It is deeply rich in diversity and yet it is the message of one mind, God's mind to us, and thereby has an inherent unity and coherence. We are to take it as a whole. As such, each of the parts is to be seen in relation to the whole. Unclear passages are to be understood in the light of those that are clear. All Scriptural teaching is to be interpreted in terms that are consistent with the teachings of Christ and the law and gospel. One should always look for parallel passages that balance or clarify or illuminate a passage.

4) *Apply it to one's life.* The study of Scripture ought never to be only academic. The purpose of the Bible is for our training and equipping in righteousness. The Bible is not just information. It is given for our salvation and moral guidance in life. We are to understand it, yes, but then press on and apply it and act upon it so that we are not just hearers only but doers of the Word. The message of the Bible enters our minds. It then must trickle down into our hearts. As it does so, we are to allow the Bible to mold our entire outlook on life, to shape our mentality, to seep in and form us.

What is important to remember here is that whereas a passage has ultimately one meaning, it can have many applications. We might be able to agree on a meaning but what does it mean to me? That can be varied and different for each person. So we are to seek for practical application, which though varied, must be consistent with the meaning of the passage.

It is important as we turn to the biblical texts that are under discussion in the debate over same-sex intercourse that we understand the task at hand. The task is to ascertain the intended meaning of the authors of the passages. God has communicated His message and will to us through the words of these passages. There is an inherent meaning in the texts. But we acknowledge the difficulties and seek to bridge the gap and remove our glasses so that we might put ourselves in the shoes of someone to whom these Scriptures were written in that day. This task involves both exegesis and hermeneutics and we ask the Holy Spirit who inspired the biblical writers to give understanding to us today that we may apply these teachings to our lives.

# SEVEN
# The Heterosexual Norm

Beginnings are important. They define categories and meaning. That's why when we desire to know what the Bible has to say about human sexuality, marriage, and same-sex unions and behavior, the place to begin is with creation. As we shall see that is where Jesus began.

It is in the creation narratives where the meaning of human sexuality is given. In these opening chapters of the Book of Genesis, we find God's creative intention for human sexuality. This intention reveals the normative pattern for that sexuality. It is in light of this normative pattern that all subsequent passages touching on heterosexuality and homosexuality are to be seen and understood. The specific reason why these early chapters are so important for the questions surrounding homosexuality is because of the all important distinctions they make between sexual differentiation, sexual (gender) identity, sexual roles and sexual preference.

Too often I find discussions and studies on homosexuality starting in a different place. They start by looking at the few places in Scripture where homosexual acts are mentioned. A lot of time is then spent on discussing the meaning of these passages and whether or not they have anything to say concerning the rightness or wrongness of homosexual behavior today. It is not that these few passages are unimportant. They are important, and we will be dealing with them at significant length as well. But they are not central. By making them the central focus, authors, gay advocates and study documents on the issue have tended to not properly examine and give due weight to the creation accounts. When the passages containing homosexual activity are examined without due reference to the wider biblical context of creation and the Fall, the categories and meanings can become blurred very quickly.

## The Creation Accounts

When Jesus was asked whether it was lawful to divorce one's wife, he took his questioners behind the Law of Moses with which he had been confronted, all the way back to creation. He reached back first to Genesis 1:27 and said, *"Have you not read that the one who made them at the beginning 'made them male and female,"* and in the next breath he reached for Genesis 2:24 and quoted an utterance that he says God himself said, *"For this reason a man shall leave his father and mother and be joined to his wife, and the two shall become one flesh"?* He finishes by adding his own commentary, *"So they are no longer two, but one flesh. Therefore what God has joined together, let no one separate".* (Matthew 19:6)

The reason why both Jesus' quotations from Genesis and his teaching in Matthew 19 is so important and central to the current discussion on human sexuality is because Jesus is the final authority for Christians. Christians are called by their Lord to believe and obediently follow what he teaches. What the Christian is confronted with in Jesus' reaching back to the creation accounts is that Jesus Christ, the incarnate Son of God, who claimed divine authority for all that he taught and did, both confirmed the absolute authority of the Old Testament for others and submitted to it unreservedly himself. It is precisely because Jesus is the final authority for Christians that Christians are bound to acknowledge the authority of Scripture as Jesus himself did.

Far from being formal citations of a convenient proof-text, then, Jesus' references to the creation accounts of Genesis were affirmations of an ordering of reality that was clearly held to be of fundamental importance. This ordering of reality was God's intention for the human race he had just created. Creation both exists by God and is ordered by

God, a product of His will. There is purpose built into the very structure of the cosmos. God's intention is that one man and one woman would know and experience the goodness of creation and sexuality within the order of marriage.

In the current debate swirling around the question of the rightness or wrongness of same- sex intercourse, proponents of same-sex relationships make much of the "silence" of Jesus regarding homosexual behavior. It is pointed out that in the Gospels Jesus makes no statement concerning the morality of same-sex intercourse. Therefore, it is quickly concluded, Jesus is of no help in shedding light on the discussion.

Nothing could be further from the truth. It is true that as with many other important subjects Jesus made no direct or explicit comments on same-sex intercourse. But in a much deeper and more important wider sense, Jesus was not "silent" about same-sex intercourse inasmuch as his perspective on marriage speaks loud and clear.[1] Imagine a totally dark and enclosed room with a single rectangular skylight in the roof on a bright, sunny day. The sun's rays would shine only directly on a rectangular area on the floor of that room beneath the skylight. However, those same rays would indirectly bring light to the entire room. In the same way, Jesus' teaching on marriage gives direct and clear teaching on marriage. But that teaching also sheds light indirectly on all matters of human sexuality. Jesus' view of Genesis 1-2, then, is foundational for a Christian view of human sexuality.

Jesus' response to the Pharisees begins by affirming that when God created human beings (represented by the collective noun "Man") in his own image, he created male *and* female. These words immediately repudiate the old myths of the androgynous (bisexual or unisexual) Man and all ambiguity in the relationship between the sexes is removed. Man is not just a sexual unity. Man is a sexual diversity. There is a sexual differentiation within Man. Man is properly understood when seen as 'male and female.' It is not man and man, or woman and woman, but man and woman. As created by God, then, Man is heterosexual by nature.

This sexual differentiation within Man is biological. An XY chromosome combination is a boy and an XX chromosome combination a girl. Genetically, we are born either male or female. Our maleness and femaleness is God-given and God-ordered. We are one or the other. It should be mentioned here, however, that even this biological sexual differentiation has been disordered by the fall of humans into sin. We know of cases where indistinct genitalia belonging to both sexes (hermaphrodite) are combined in one individual. But this condition is extremely rare and the result of the abnormality and disorder of a fallen world. From the beginning, God differentiated human beings sexually as male *and* female.

From creation, however, there is something even prior to our creation as male and female. From creation gender precedes sex. By 'gender' we mean masculine and feminine, a wider concept than sex, more like "lifestyle" or "emotional identity". God is Spirit. As such there is no physical or sexual aspect to God. But masculine and feminine gender is rooted in the very nature of God. So when Adam and Eve are created in the image of God, that image is the pattern for their sexual nature. There is an emotional identity in God which is the pattern for our sexual nature as male and female. This gender pattern is our true gender identity. This is who God sees us as being. Gender is a given. It is given in the most secure and purposeful way possible, in the very image of God Himself. It is a gift from God. Adam and Eve's gender identities were consistent with their biological sex—their sexual identity as male and female.

God created the human being in his image. This is the wonder of Man. Unlike any other part of God's creation, the plurality in humankind reflects the plurality of God. His image is not reflected in the man alone, not in man with man or woman with woman, but in man and woman together. The primal form of humanity is thus the togetherness of man and woman. To be human is to share humanity with the opposite sex.[2]

With God creating Man by nature heterosexual, God at the same time has put the totality of marriage in nature and not just sexual capability itself. Marriage is the work of God and therefore his creation. It is God who joins a man and woman together in marriage—whether they realize it or not. Marriage is, as both Jesus and Paul speak of it, a gift. It is not something achieved (although it surely must be worked at!). It is not achieved either through procreation or through developing a quality relationship. It is not the relationship in either its social or sexual aspects that creates the marriage. It is more that the marriage creates the relationship.[3] Thus marriage, the exclusive life-long commitment of one man and one woman, is the place for sexual activity.

Our true nature then is not what presently exists, but what God originally created and intended. After the fall, the nature that existed was no longer pure. Neither human beings nor the created earth escaped the curse. Identity, sexuality, and all the created order are now broken and disordered. Nowhere does nature now reflect the perfect will of God, and the divine intent can never be established merely by observing human behavior. That is why our true nature as human beings cannot be known apart from revelation nor separated from the Doctrine of creation.

The Genesis creation account teaches that Man is not only heterosexual by nature but that there are no other distinctions in the human race. Mankind is one kind. All other distinctions in the human race—racial, cultural, linguistic - arose after the fall. There is only one sexual differentiation recorded before the fall, the differentiation between male and female. This is the great heterosexual divide. And because of its central importance in the current discussions of homosexuality, we note that this heterosexual divide is one of *kind* not quality. The further division related to heterosexual and homosexual is a result of the fall. Sin disrupts God's order and homosexuality bears witness to that disruption. Homosexuality, then, has its origins not in creation but in the fall.

It is clear from the creation narrative that Man is the crown of God's creation. To Man is given the privilege and joy of obeying God's mandate to be fruitful, to multiply and to have dominion over God's creation. God blessed them and said to them, *"Be fruitful and multiply, and fill the earth and subdue it*". (Genesis 1:28) However, the main purpose for God creating them male and female was not that they would be more efficient in carrying out God's mandate, but that through them God creates companionship and community. Being created "male and female" is connected more closely to being created in God's image than to the blessing that follows, to "be fruitful and multiply." (v. 28) Sexuality is not essential to Man's relationship with God.

This centrality of companionship is underscored in the second chapter. God puts Adam into the garden to till it and keep it and then says, *"It is not good that the man should be alone; I will make him a helper as his partner"*. (vv. 15 &18) Here is God's first ever negative judgment. Up to this point God had pronounced everything good. Here now is something that is not good. Man is alone and isolated. The cattle and birds and animals of the field are no solution for Adam's aloneness. So God, whose all-seeing eye penetrated to the depth of Adam's aloneness, causes a deep sleep to fall upon him. God takes one of Adam's ribs and builds it into a woman and brings her to Adam. Here now was one who was the same as he (*"bone of my bone and flesh of my flesh"*) and yet different from him (*"this one shall be called Woman"*). Once again, there is no bisexual or unisexual ideal here. Rather, there is a constitutional distinction in the being of man as woman is created from him. Out of the undifferentiated humanity of Man, male and female emerged. It would not be another man that would fulfill man's desire for human fulfillment, but someone who was a part of himself and yet distinctively 'other'. In fabulous imagery, God displays his purpose of human companionship, complementarity, and intimacy between man and woman.

The man and woman are not the same, they are diverse. And yet, in sexual intercourse they are not diverse, but become the same, "one flesh". There is a powerful sexual desire of the male and female toward each other. It is a desire stronger than the tie to one's parents, a desire that clings inwardly toward each other and a desire that will not rest. It comes from the fact that God took the woman out of the man and that they were originally *one* flesh. The sex drive inherent in their creation by God moves them to come together again, for they belong to each other. As they consummate their love for each other in sexual intercourse, they return to that original oneness.

The 'one flesh' union of the man and woman is established by sexual intercourse. It is a complementarity that is grounded in, and fully embraces, our bodies and their structures. But becoming 'one flesh' is more than just the physical union. The complementarity of male and female sexual organs is only a symbol at the physical level of a much deeper spiritual complement. 'One flesh' involves the whole being and affects the personality at the deepest level. It is the union of the whole man and the whole woman. In that union they become distinctly 'one', wholly different and set apart from other human relational unities, such as the family or the race.

Becoming "one flesh" in sexual intercourse also has a procreative purpose. In Genesis 1 we read that God blessed the man and the woman and said to them, *"Be fruitful and multiply"*. Through the oneness of sexual intercourse, the man and woman become procreators. In procreation we create for, or on behalf of *(pro-)*, the Creator of all things. The wonder of wonders is that God has chosen to create new human beings by means of human procreators who were created in his image. As God created male and female in the beginning, we now have been given the great commission of being present with God as procreators at the beginning of new human life. Through the mysterious participation of our procreative powers in God's own creative work, we transmit life to those who will succeed us.

Becoming "one flesh" in intercourse then expresses two things: a strengthening of love and the production of children. In the mystery of our beings as men and women, God has joined these two things together. He joined together the quality of relationship *and* the kind of relationship. In the beginning, God joined together the relational and the procreative purposes of sex and marriage.

As Jesus reaches back to the creation accounts in his reply to the Pharisees, we learn at least four things about the nature of this marriage union.

**1)** *First, marriage is an exclusive relationship.* It is to be the union of one man and one woman. It is exclusive as to kind. It is not to be that of a man with another man, or a woman with another woman. In the beginning, God *created* humankind in his own image, male and female he created them. At the beginning, God *brought* the first woman to the first man, much as today the bride's father brings the bride to the groom, thereby establishing a norm for the human race. Judaism and Christianity did not invent the heterosexual norm. God did. It was in his mind from the beginning. It was his intention that this exclusive union of the man and woman be the foundation of all human community.

**2)** *Second, marriage is a publicly recognized relationship.* It is not just a private arrangement between two individuals. There is a societal dimension to marriage. There is public recognition involved. Society has a vested interest in marriage. This public *"leaving"* of a man's parents in order to form a new family unit varies in custom and detail from culture to culture. But the principle of a man and his wife becoming as one and having special rights to each other is to be found everywhere.

**3)** *Third, marriage is a committed relationship.* The man leaves his father and mother and he is joined to, united with, *cleaves* to his wife. Marriage is a loving, cleaving commitment. It is a relationship that requires commitments that go well beyond the demands of personal satisfaction. Marriage is a place where a fear of commitment is overcome and where we are to learn to place another person's needs before our own. It is commitment first to one's spouse. It is a commitment then to one's children and the creating of an environment in which the next generation can flourish. It is a commitment to society which gives support to family life as the basis for the structure of society.

**4)** *Fourth, marriage is a permanent relationship.* The man and woman become *"one flesh"*. In consummating their love in sexual intercourse, the man and woman are reunited in the oneness of their creation. Sexual intercourse is a sign and seal of the marriage covenant. The Creator has instilled within us the deep desire for an enduring relationship. In the permanence of this relationship the human being is truly 'completed' or fulfilled. This life-long union between a man and his wife is the teaching Jesus would later endorse to which he added, *"What God has joined together, let man not separate"*.

## The Fall

But this is not the last word that can be found concerning marriage and sexuality in these early chapters of Genesis. We need to look further into Genesis 3 where we learn what happens when humans try to find fulfillment outside the boundaries and permissions established by God. The man and woman are tempted to live beyond these permissions and to live according to their own will. They disobey God. The result of this disobedience, which is commonly called the Fall, is tragic in every area of life. There is separation of the man from the woman which is represented by covering their nakedness. There is separation from God represented by hiding among the trees of the Garden. Human beings now live alienated from God, themselves, each other and nature. All is spoiled. Now the sexual roles of the pair are confused and disordered. Genesis 3:16 descriptively shows that now the relationship between the man and woman will be servility and domination instead of full companionship.

One of the results of the fall is sexual role disorder. In a fallen world God describes for the woman what the reality will be: *"Your desire shall be for your husband, and he shall rule over you"*. (Genesis 3:16) God is describing here what will be; not prescribing what ought to be. Things are not now as they were. The sexual role disorder does not, however, necessarily produce sexual identity disorder. The woman still perceives herself to be a woman and the man still perceives himself to be a man because they were conscious of their nakedness. The image of God in them, although spoiled and marred and twisted, was not obliterated or destroyed. They still retained their given sexuality or gender differentiation as God had created them male and female. However, in this broken world, the way they will live out their sexual roles will not be the way God originally intended. Instead of mutuality, there will be subservience.

In this abnormal and broken world, there is also sexual preference disorder. Here is where we come to a basic understanding of the homosexual condition. The homosexual desire to find a loving relationship with another of his or her own sex is real and can be extremely strong. The sexual desire itself is God-created and proper but it has become disordered. Something has gone wrong. This disordered desire is not a desire placed in a man or woman from creation. It is a misdirected desire that has arisen since the fall and is the result of the brokenness of the fallenness of humankind. In its misdirection, the homosexual desire is a desire directed toward another who is a reflection of one's self. It is a desire that does not return the homosexual person to the 'one flesh' of an original oneness with one who is a different gender. For this reason homosexual behavior is explicitly and consistently repudiated by God. Homosexual acts violate God's intention that man and woman should constitute one flesh in which his image is reflected.

God's intention for his creation is not polygamy and polyandry which infringe the one man—one woman principle; it is not hidden unions since these have not involved a public leaving of parents; it is not casual encounters and temporary liaisons, adultery and many divorces which are incompatible with 'cleaving' and with Jesus' prohibition 'let man not separate'; it is not homosexual partnerships which violate the statement that 'a man' shall be joined to 'his wife'. All these sexual disorders have resulted from man's rebellion against God and are symptomatic of the bondage to sin that engulfs all people. The only 'one flesh' experience that God intends and Scripture contemplates is the sexual union of a man with his wife whom he recognizes as 'flesh of his flesh'.

The doctrine of the Fall is not given its due weight in the current debate. Yet it is crucial to a true understanding of God and man. The reality of the true historic Fall means that the world of pain and suffering and disorder that we perceive and experience is not a true reflection of God's character and love. All these things are abnormalities in God's world rather than a part of God's original intention for his creation. The Fall is a crucial strength for the Christian. If we had to believe that the world, as it now is, is the way God made it and wanted it to be, then it would be virtually impossible to believe God is good. If we had to believe that the homosexual condition, wrought with its pain and loneliness and suffering, is the way God made us and wanted us to be, then it would be very difficult to love God. For our integrity as Christians, it is extremely important that we know that the biblical view of the Fall is true. It means that God is not the author of the pain and suffering and injustice and evil. The source of the suffering and evil in this world is rebellious human choice. With regard to the homosexual condition, because God is not the author of sexual disorders, we can fight against these disorders without fighting God. We need not resign ourselves to any of the results of the fall, but we are to fight against the thorns and thistles, sin and suffering, sickness and death.

### The Biblical Narrative Stream

In appealing to the Genesis creation accounts, Jesus reaffirms the heterosexual norm for marriage. In the rest of the Scriptures, prohibitions that forbid sexual practices that deviate from this sexual norm are fences of protection around that original creation ordinance. Indeed, the *negative* prohibitions against homosexual practice make sense only in the light of its *positive* teaching in Genesis 1 - 2 about human sexuality and heterosexual marriage.

The question then arises: Did Jesus uphold these fences around marriage or did he tear them down? What did Jesus do with the moral law?

God erected the tallest fence around marriage and human sexuality in Exodus 20:14 in the words of the Sixth Commandment, *"You shall not commit adultery"*. The institution of marriage was so central and important to God that he established one of the Ten Commandments for its protection. This commandment protects the sacredness of marriage by forbidding any sexual practice that in any way threatens marriage: adultery, incest, homosexuality, bestiality.

In addition to affirming the creation accounts and the heterosexual norm, Jesus also upheld the Mosaic Law. He did prioritize the law's core and even amended the law by closing loopholes and expanding its demands. (Matt. 5:21-48)[5] But at no time did Jesus overturn a specific prohibition of the moral law. Quite the contrary, Jesus said, *"Do not think that I have come to abolish the law or the prophets; I have come not to abolish but to fulfill...not one tiny iota or one tiny letter stroke shall pass away from the law until all things come to pass"*. (Matt. 5:17-18) Jesus' "silence" on the matter of homosexual behavior as such indicates his acceptance of the teachings of the Old Testament which we will see is unanimous in its rejection of same-sex intercourse.

The Apostle Paul follows Jesus in affirming the creation accounts and heterosexual norm. In Ephesians 5, Paul gives his general teaching on marriage and the family. And what an extraordinary teaching it is! Paul believes that one's relationship to Jesus Christ is to transform all other relationships of life. In this passage he speaks of how one's relationship to Christ is to work itself out within the husband-wife relationship in marriage.

In Christ there is and is to be an overcoming of the sexual role disorder of the Fall. Husbands and wives are to be subject to one another out of reverence for Christ. (v. 21) Husbands are to love their wives. Wives are to love their husbands. If a husband ever wonders what is to be the nature of this love for his wife, he is encouraged to look to Christ and understand how it is that Christ loved his bride, the Church. Christ served and loved her even unto death. If a wife ever wonders what is to be the nature of this love for her husband, she is encouraged to look to the Church and understand how it is that the Church is to love Christ. The Church is to submit to Christ as an expression of love, a love that is met by a love that is willing to sacrifice itself for the beloved.

The entire passage is a meditation on marriage as a sacramental sign of the union of Christ and his Church. Just as in the Old Testament, God is seen as the husband of his bride Israel, so here Christ is seen as the Bridegroom of his bride the Church. The husband is to nourish and love his wife as his own body just as Christ loves and nourishes his own body the Church. The reason is because they are "one flesh."

In verse 31 Paul, as did Jesus, reaches back and draws on the creation account of a man leaving father and mother and becoming "one flesh" with her. At this, Paul is caught up in the wonder of it all. You can almost see him set down his pen, gaze out the window and say, "Christ's love for the Church and her response of love for him is the model for marriage! The Genesis passage contains a prophecy of Christ's marriage to his bride the Church, a prophecy whose meaning had been hidden but which now is revealed! The love of husband and wife helps to make understandable the love of Christ for the Church. And the love of Christ for the Church helps make understandable the love of husband and wife. How marvelous!" But this "oneness" of husband and wife, Christ and Church, is a deep mystery. Who indeed can plummet to the depths of the mystery of oneness!

Once again there is a drawing on the heterosexual norm in the creation accounts. This time it is Paul seeing it as a sign of the union of Christ and his Church.

To the very end of the Scriptures, this heterosexual model is seen as the norm. In Revelation 19:7 & 9 there is great rejoicing in heaven, *"for the marriage of the Lamb has come, and his bride has made herself ready. Blessed are those who are invited to the marriage supper of the Lamb"*.

From the creation accounts in Genesis to the marriage supper of the Lamb and his Church in Revelation, the whole stream of Holy Scripture assumes the heterosexual, monogamous norm, despite the fact of royal and patriarchal polygamy. In this narrative stream, two things stand out. The entire narrative stream wholeheartedly celebrates human sexuality as a gift. But in its genital expression, it is reserved for heterosexual marriage within which it is to be enjoyed and desired:

> "Drink water from your own cistern, flowing water from your own well. . . . Let your fountain be blessed, and rejoice in the wife of your youth, a lovely deer, a graceful doe. May her breasts satisfy you at all times; may you be *intoxicated always by her love."*
> (Proverbs. 5:15-19)

"How fair and pleasant you are, O loved one, delectable maiden! You are stately as a palm tree, and your breasts are like its clusters. I say I will climb the palm tree and lay hold of its branches. O may your breasts be like clusters of the vine, and the scent of your breath like apples, and your kisses like the best wine that goes down smoothly, gliding over lips and teeth. I am my beloved's and his desire is for me. Come, my beloved, let us go forth into the fields and lodge in the villages . . . There I will give you *my love.*" (Song of Solomon 7:6-12)

# EIGHT

## Old Testament
## Biblical Fences Around Marriage

### Genesis 19:1-11

The first Old Testament fence around marriage that is most often cited in connection with homosexual behavior is Genesis 19:1-11.

In this passage we read the notorious story of the men of Sodom which has been widely understood by Christians to be a condemnation of homosexual practice. An outcry regarding the great sinfulness of the city had come before God. (Gen. 18:20-21) God sets out to investigate the truthfulness of these allegations by sending two companions (angels) to the city. Upon arriving at Sodom in the evening, they meet Lot who invites them to spend the night in his house. At first the guests decline the offer, but eventually accept the invitation and, as was the custom, Lot shows them wonderful hospitality, providing an abundant meal and shelter.

But before they retire for the evening, the men of the city surround the house and demand that Lot *"bring them out to us, so that we may know them,"* (Gen. 19:5) or *"so we can have sex with them"*. (NIV) Unwilling to do so, Lot pleads with them not to act so wickedly. He tries to bargain with them by offering his two daughters instead. But the men of Sodom are not interested in Lot's daughters, become angry with him and shout, *"Stand back! This fellow came here as an alien, and he would play the judge! Now we will deal worse with you than with them"*. (Gen. 19:9) The angels rescue Lot from the mob and Lot and his family are brought out of the city and told to flee for their lives.

Nobody challenges the fact that the men of Sodom were wicked and were sinning greatly against the Lord. The question is: "What was or were the sins of Sodom?"

## New Approach and Arguments

The new approach which challenges the traditional exegesis of this text is put forth powerfully by the Yale historian John Boswell in his book, *Christianity, Social Tolerance, and Homosexuality.* (1980) This book has been extremely influential and widely read and quoted by many people since being published. Boswell represents a group that objects to the Church's traditional understanding that the sin of Sodom was homosexual acts. He says this is really an unfair reading of the text. Boswell argues that,

> "Lot was violating the custom of Sodom . . . by entertaining unknown guests within the city walls at night without obtaining the permission of the elders of the city. When the men of Sodom gathered around to demand that the strangers be brought out to them 'that they may *know* them,' they meant no more than to 'know' who they were, and the city was consequently destroyed not for sexual immorality but for the sin of inhospitality to strangers."[1]

So Boswell and others are saying that when the men of Sodom demand that Lot bring the angels out to them, they were not demanding to 'know' them in the sense of having sex with them, but in order to become acquainted with them. They did not want sex with them. Rather, they merely wanted to carry out the custom of the city and show hospitality to the strangers. The implication is that Lot was guilty of a serious breech of hospitality because he had not introduced the two strangers to the other men of the city. This breech of hospitality was the major sin, not homosexuality.

Boswell points out that the Hebrew word 'to know' (*yadha'*) occurs 943 times in the Old Testament and only 10 times does it clearly mean to have sex. For example, Adam knew his wife Eve (Gen. 4:1, 17, 25) and she conceived. Obviously, he was not just "getting acquainted" with her!

Boswell argues, then, that the sin here is the breech of hospitality. He and others point out that there are numerous other references in the Old Testament—and a few in the New Testament - to the sins of Sodom and argue that homosexual practice is never clearly and explicitly identified as one of them. Sodom was destroyed, according to Boswell, because of the sin of inhospitality. Any claim, then, that the story is a blanket condemnation of homosexual practice in general is unjustified. Boswell's interpretation of the Sodom incident in terms of hospitality and not homosexuality is now widely influential.

## Evaluating the New Arguments

But does this argument of inhospitality really stand up under careful scrutiny? Boswell's interpretation is open to serious criticism. In the first place, it is certainly not satisfactory to decide the meaning of _yadha'_, 'to know', by statistics, otherwise the less common meaning of a word would never be probable. According to the Hebrew Lexicon of Brown Driver and Briggs, of the 943 times _yadha'_ occurs in the Old Testament, 17 refer to sexual intercourse, and 28 to 'get acquainted with'. The word has a wide range of meanings, including to know, perceive, experience, find out, discriminate, consider, be acquainted with, have sexual intercourse with, be skilful in, be wise, etc.[2] Though it is the case that of the numerous times the Hebrew word "to know" is used in the whole of the Old Testament, and only 17 times does it mean to have sex, yet seven of those times are found in Genesis and one of those seven in the very passage in question. If one were to look exclusively at the large number of times in the Old Testament the word "to know" means something other than "to have intercourse with", one might feel the weight and say Genesis 19:8 is not speaking in the sexual sense. But meaning of words must be determined by context. Only the immediate context can decide meaning.

No one denies the sexual connotations of Lot offering his daughters to the crowd of men in place of the two guests. In this very clear sexual context Lot says, _"Look, I have two daughters who have not known a man"_. (v. 8) In other words, Lot's daughters were virgins. They had not had sexual intercourse. The men of Sodom demand "to know" the two male guests. Lot offers his two daughters so that the men of Sodom can "know them". The context here strongly implies that the men of Sodom were demanding to have sex with Lot's visitors. The context here is one of gang rape essentially. It is not, as many have pointed out, a situation of consenting adults who want to do this thing together. This context is different. These two visitors come to Lot and are taken in by him. The men of the city—young and old—come and demand to have sex with them. Lot pleads with them not to act so wickedly. Lot hopes to appease them with the offer of his virgin daughters instead. This willingness raises obvious questions about Lot's righteousness and fatherly love and protectiveness, but what seems clear are the sexual intentions of the men of the city.

Secondly, it is difficult to understand how Sodom's punishment is commensurate with the 'sin of Sodom' seen in terms only of rules of hospitality. Advocates for the new and revised interpretation are right in emphasizing that hospitality was very important in the ancient world. It was a part of the fabric of custom and culture. But it is hard to square language like "wicked" (Gen. 19:7) and "grievous" (Gen. 18:20) and "detestable and vile" (Judges 19:23), if the men merely wanted to become familiar with the visitors. As important as hospitality was, it is hard to square fire and brimstone pouring down on the cities and the entire plain, destroying them and all their inhabitants, because of a breech of hospitality. Word usage and context make this revisionist argument very weak.

The argument is put forth that other biblical passages list the sins of Sodom (from which we have received the word 'sodomy'), but don't mention homosexual practice. This argument warrants a quick look at some of these later passages. Isaiah likens the deplorable condition surrounding Jerusalem to that of Sodom and Gomorrah. (Isaiah 1:7-17) He labels their offerings and incense an "abomination". Then in language reminiscent of Sodom's wickedness toward the vulnerable among them, visitors (the angels), and resident aliens (Lot), Isaiah pronounced them guilty of injustices to the oppressed, the orphan, and the widow.

Jeremiah 23:14 refers to the sins of Sodom as adultery, lying and general wickedness. So the sins of Sodom clearly were plural, not singular. Ezekiel 16:49 speaks of the sin of Sodom as arrogance, gluttony and social injustice, i.e., a failure to help the poor and needy. But the passage goes on in the next verse and talks about those who did abominable things which in both its context and use of the same word found in the Levitical prohibitions (Leviticus 18:22-20:13) for homosexual intercourse, suggests the commission of homosexual acts. In Luke 10:10-12 Jesus declares that a worse fate will befall towns that treat his messengers inhospitably than befell the city of Sodom. II Peter 2:7 links Sodom and Gomorrah with the *"filthy lives of lawless men"*. In Jude 7 a sexual aspect is explicitly stated. It says, *"In a similar way Sodom and Gomorrah and the surrounding towns gave themselves to sexual immorality and pursued unnatural lust"*. Jude 8 is linked to Jude 7, and "while sexual immorality in general is clearly indicated, a specific reference to homosexual activities can hardly be excluded".[3] The argument's main thrust is that in none of these passages is homosexual behavior explicitly linked to the Sodom story.

Two responses need to be made to this argument. First, it is far more likely that some of these later biblical passages do make implicit reference to the sin of homosexual practice than the argument is willing to concede. There is good evidence that Ezekiel in all likelihood understood the actions of the men of Sodom in light of Leviticus 18:22 and 20:13 which speak of homosexual behavior as an abomination. Both II Peter and Jude link the sin of Sodom with passions for sexual immorality, not failure to provide hospitality or social injustice. Second, it would be a mistake to conclude that because a biblical writer does not mention the specific sin of homosexual behavior, that writer would condone same-sex behavior. A writer's main focus is to make Scripture relevant to his audience. Therefore, the biblical writer would highlight the elements of the Sodom story that spoke to the issues of the day. If homosexual activity was not a concern, there would be no need to select that element from the Sodom story and address it explicitly. God judged the cities for a wide variety of sins—including homosexual practice.

Since 1955 a number of modern revisionist scholars have favored the interpretation that the sin of Sodom was inhospitality. That was the year Derrick Sherwin Bailey published his famous book, *Homosexuality and the Western Christian Tradition*. Bailey's book was the first work of serious scholarship to re-evaluate the traditional understanding of the biblical prohibitions to homosexual acts. Whether or not they accept Bailey's attempted reconstruction that the sin of Sodom was inhospitality, all subsequent writers on this topic have had to take careful account of his writing. Some writers have built on the foundations of his preliminary reconstruction a much more permissive position. However, because of the weight of the immediate context of Lot offering his two daughters and the close parallels in the story of the Levite's concubine in Judges 19:22 & 25, most scholars today do not accept Bailey's argument—even if they support same-sex behavior. In the words of one commentator, "The doubt created by Dr. Bailey has traveled more widely than the reasons he produces for it. Not one of these reasons, it may be suggested, stands any serious scrutiny".[4]

Sherwin Bailey admits that in the literature written by Jewish rabbis, Philo (20 BC - AD 50—an Alexandrian theologian) and Josephus (37/38-AD 96—an apologist and historian of the Jewish people) present the homosexual interpretation of the sin of Sodom. He claims, however, that this is uncommon in the rest of Rabbinic literature.[5] R. T. Beckwith, a scholar in this area, maintains that Bailey is completely wrong in this and quotes numerous rabbinic sources which refer to the sin of Sodom as being of the sexual nature.[6]

### The Historic-Biblical View

Long before God destroyed the city, we are told that *"the men of Sodom were wicked and sinning greatly against the Lord"* (Gen. 13:13) and that *"the outcry against Sodom and Gomorrah"* was *"so great and their sin so grievous"* (Genesis 18:20-21) that God sent the two angels to investigate the outcry of the sinfulness of Sodom that had come before Him. Abraham bargains with God like an oriental trader (Genesis 18:22-33) and gets God to agree that if even ten righteous men are found in the city, He will not destroy it. But God does not find ten righteous persons, which underscores the all pervasive wickedness of the city. God found the allegations to be true and acted in judgment against the wickedness of the people of Sodom, a wickedness which included the sin of inhospitality but which was undoubtedly exemplified by homosexual activity. So this incident was only a final confirmation of widespread sinfulness of all kinds including the habitual practice of homosexual vice already occurring. It would surely not be the case that all previous homosexual behavior in the city was characterized by forcible rape. To summarize in a way that foreshadows Paul's theological teaching in Romans 1, homosexual practice in the Sodom story appears as an illustration of the all pervasive pagan wickedness, idolatry and immorality of the city which brings upon itself the wrath and judgment of a righteous God within the wider context of the general ungodliness of a post-Fall world.

But someone may still ask, "Is it not homosexual rape that is being condemned in the Sodom story? All can agree that such rape is terribly wrong. But can we be sure that this story is positively against homosexual behavior as such?" Certain theologians make the argument that this Genesis passage does not provide strong argument against prohibiting all homosexual acts. It is argued that the passage says nothing at all about the morality of consensual relations between persons of the same sex. Therefore, this story has little or no relevance to the Church's current discussions.

I think the proper response to these questions and conclusion is that it depends on the framework within which one is operating. If one is examining this passage within its immediate historical setting only, I think the argument makes a valid point. If one is looking at the leaf of the tree only, with a blind eye toward the branch, the limb, the trunk and the roots, the argument can stand. In that isolated historical context, the passage does not provide strong argument against prohibiting homosexual behavior as such. But can one explain the leaf rightly without understanding the roots, trunk, limb and branch on which it has grown? If one sees it in the wider context of the Biblical revelation on human sexuality in Genesis 1-2, then it can be understood as including homosexual acts of whatever kind being against the heterosexual norm for sexuality established by God in creation. The early chapters of Genesis not only provide the foundation for biblical sexual ethics, but supply the interpretive framework within which all passages that follow are to be understood, including the story of Sodom.

### Judges 19:22-25

There is a very similar story to the Sodom story in Judges 19.

A Levite and his concubine were traveling from Bethlehem in Judah to Ephraim when they came at nightfall to Gibeah. An old man returning from his day's work in the field sees them in the open square of the city and invites them into his house for the night. While they were enjoying a generous meal, the men of the city, a perverse lot they are called, surround the house and demand of the old man, *"Bring out the man who came into your house, so that we may know him"*, (v. 22) or *"have sex them him"*. (NIV) The old man pleads with them not to act so wickedly, not to do such a vile thing. He even offers his daughter and his visitor's concubine as a bribe saying, *"Ravish them and do whatever you want to them"*. (v. 24) But they would not listen to him so the man gave them his concubine and they wantonly raped her and abused her all through the night.

### New Approach and Arguments

As in the case of the Sodom story, those who take the new approach argue that when the men of Gibeah demand that the old man bring out to them the Levite, they are not demanding to 'know' him in a sexual sense, but in order to get acquainted with him. It is argued that the story is emphasizing "the deplorable lack of courtesy shown by the Gibeathites toward the visitor".[7] There is therefore, according to Bailey, no reason to suspect the men of Gibeah of homosexual behavior. God punished the people of Gibeah for breeching the rules of hospitality, not for threatening homosexual assault.

## Evaluating the New Arguments

Does this argument bear close scrutiny? Once again, the crux of the meaning of this story centers on the exact meaning of the men's demands to bring out the visitors so that they can "know" them. A close look at word usage and context strongly support a connotation of sexual violence.

As we have seen, there is little question in the story of Sodom that when Lot offers his daughters, it is talking about having sex with them. Here in Judges, when the old man offers his daughter and the visitor's concubine, the old man clearly offers them to the men of the city for their sexual pleasure.

Genesis 19:8 *"I have two daughters who have not known a man."*

Judges 19:25 *"and they knew her."*

It seems clear from the context and from the same word usage *(yadha')* that this incident also is speaking clearly of homosexual assault.

Genesis 19:5b *"Bring them out to us that we may know them."*

Judges 19:22d *"Bring out the man who came into your house, that we may know him."*

Virtually all theologians up until recently have understood and accepted the phrase *"that we may know him"*, as describing so vile a thing that it refers to sexual assault. The man here in Judges replies, *"don't be so vile"*. (v. 23) Although a breech of hospitality was gravely serious, this response seems out of sorts to protest a breech of hospitality as opposed to rape. It certainly makes no sense if the men merely wanted to become familiar with the man. Bailey's interpretation is well-intentioned and in many ways ingenious but unconvincing since it fails to do justice to the immediate context.

The Historic-Biblical View.

As we look at these stories of Sodom and Gibeah, it needs to be reiterated that those who argue for a revised way of understanding these texts rightly have drawn our attention to the fact that Sodom and Gomorrah were guilty of a huge range of sins. Throughout the Bible Sodom is used as a metaphor for God's righteous judgment on radical godlessness and idolatry. The prophets and New Testament writers identify the sins of Sodom as hatred of authority, greed, pride, immorality of all sorts, idolatry, injustice, shamelessness, deception, complacency, luxury and ease leading to the neglect and exploitation of the poor, violation of hospitality as well as extravagant lust after strange flesh. So Sodom's sin was far more than just sexual sin which in part was an expression of the chaos and debasement of the times and culture. It does show a biased reading of the Scriptures, then, if we identify the sin of Sodom exclusively with homosexuality.

But most students of the Bible, because of the usage of language and context, agree with the Church's longstanding understanding and have accepted that sexual sin and spe-cifically homosexual sin was involved. It was one of the sins that came forth from their radical idolatry and godlessness. Those who dismiss homosexual behavior altogether as one of Sodom's sins do real injustice to the text.

The only argument in my mind that has any persua-siveness comes from those who say that the sin of Sodom does not address the possibility of loving, monogamous, homosexual partnerships. It is argued that the sin was the abusive, violent intentions of the men to gang rape Lot's visitors. If this passage was the only reference to homo-sexual acts in the Bible, it would not resolve the question of whether or not homosexual behavior in and of itself is intrinsically wrong, irrespective of context. But it is not the only passage we have. We are to read this story as we have read the Sodom story not only within the wider context of the creation accounts, but also the other passages that follow.

**Leviticus 18 & 20**

We move on to the Book of Leviticus, the 18th and 20th chapters. These chapters are found within what is commonly known as the Holiness Code (Leviticus 17-26) which is the heart of the book. The Holiness Code challenges the people of God to follow his laws and not copy the practices either of Egypt (where they used to live) or of Canaan (to which he was bringing them). There are two passages within this larger block of laws that mention homosexual acts.

Leviticus 18:22 *"You shall not lie with a male as with a woman; it is an abomination."*

Leviticus 20:13 *"If a man lies with a male as with a woman, both of them have committed an abomination: they shall be put to death; their blood is upon them."*

As we come to these passages, it is important to recognize the practices of the nations and cultures surrounding Israel at the time with regard to homosexual behavior. In contrast to the Hittites in Mesopotamia and the Egyptians and Canaanites in Asia Minor, the Old Testament laws on homosexuality stand out strikingly. The cultures of the ancient Orient surrounding Israel viewed homosexual acts as quite acceptable within certain limits, provided they were not incestuous or forcible. In sharp contrast, the Old Testament and these Levitical Laws appear to ban all homosexual acts—even where both parties freely consent.

In both these passages we note that the word used to describe the act of *"a man lying with a man as one lies with a woman"* is the word 'abomination'. The word 'abomination' in Hebrew *(to'evah)* is a special designation. It connotes something more serious than breaking a Jewish law or custom. *"To'evah"* comes from the root meaning of the word "to hate" or "to abhor". An abomination is literally something detestable and hated by God. It is a very strong word. It is used to refer to something horrific. It is a word that implies incompatibility with the nature of the Creator himself, a reversal of what was intended. It is a word used in such contexts as offering children to idols (Leviticus

18:21) and male prostitution involving idolatry (I Kings 14:24). It is a very, very strong term of condemnation.

## New Approach and Arguments

Those who would revise the traditional understanding at this point are in agreement that there is no doubt that the Levitical Holiness Code prohibits the act of homosexual intercourse. The Levitical texts are straightforward, unqualified and unambiguous. However, some of them would argue that in its context the prohibitions apply only to pagan and perhaps cultic homosexual practices, not to homosexual relations in general. It was the presence of male prostitutes in the land that was condemned. God's prohibition against same-sex practices, it is argued, spoke of his judgment against idolatry and this prohibition does not speak against physical lovemaking by two loving, committed homosexuals in our day.

Boswell and Bailey and others who follow them believe these Old Testament laws are part of Israel's purity code, an elaborate system of ritual "cleanliness" whereby the Jews would be distinguished from neighboring peoples. As such, these purity codes were important for Israel but are irrelevant for Christians today. In commenting on the Holiness Code in their book, *Is The Homosexual My Neighbor?*, Scanzoni and Mollenkott note that it includes commandments 'not to eat meat with blood in it, not to wear garments made of two kinds of yarn, not to plant fields with two kinds of seed' and so on. They then draw the conclusion:

> "Consistency and fairness would seem to dictate that if the Israelite Holiness Code is to be invoked against twentieth-century homosexuals, it should likewise be invoked against such common practices as eating rare steak, wearing mixed fabrics, and having marital intercourse during the menstrual period."[8]

These authors are saying that if you are going to reject these other laws which are there in the Levitical Law, such as having intercourse during the menstrual period, then we must also reject the laws about homosexuality. These Levitical Laws, it is said, are not laws that stand for all time. Thus, it is argued, we are not dealing with moral absolutes here, with the intrinsic wrongness of homosexual acts. It is the context of pagan idolatry that makes them wrong. We are dealing with an outdated purity code that is no longer morally binding. As Boswell states, "the Levitical enactments against homosexual behavior characterize it unequivocally unclean rather than inherently evil".[8]

Boswell writes that the Hebrew word *'to'evah'* does not usually signify something intrinsically evil like rape or theft. Rather, it signifies something that is ritually unclean for the Jews like eating pork or engaging in intercourse during menstruation. He contends that it is used throughout the Old Testament to designate those Jewish sins that involve ethnic contamination or idolatry.

Boswell further claims that almost no early Church Fathers appealed to Leviticus as authority against homosexual acts.[10] But David Wright of Edinburgh, a New Testament scholar critiquing Boswell's work, says at this point there is no evidence that Boswell has checked approximately 140 references to these texts in the first three volumes of *Biblia Patristica*. Boswell does cite Clement of Alexandria as an exception as well as the fourth century work *Apostolic Constitutions*. Wright states that while Leviticus 18 and 20 are not widely cited in Christian literature in the early centuries, they are cited not as rarely as Boswell makes out.[11] So Boswell and Bailey would say that these prohibitions are part of the older ceremonial, sacrificial, Jewish ritual laws that don't need to be kept today.

### Evaluating the New Arguments

With regard to the revisionist argument that the Levitical prohibitions apply only to pagan fertility rites, it must be pointed out that they cite no good reason why the prohibitions would not apply to other instances. Also, the fact that both participants are to be punished (Leviticus. 20:13) would lead one to conclude that at least sometimes the prohibited sex was consensual. In the words *"as with a woman"* it would seem that one is confronted again with the perspective of the Genesis creation accounts. God intends that sexual activity take place within the heterosexual norm he established.

Now obviously when one looks at the Old Testament, it is important to ask what laws still do apply to us today. If you have been in conversations on this matter, you undoubtedly have heard someone say, "Christians are no longer under the Old Testament law. Christ is the end of the law. Christians are now under Christ, not the law". Or again, "Christians break other Old Testament laws all the time such as eating pork and lobster. To pick and choose and follow some laws and break others is being grossly inconsistent". On the surface, these seem like formidable problems. But their proposed answer—the abandonment of the relevance of the Old Testament—is not the only course. The more difficult and essential task is to go beneath the surface and look more closely at the Old Testament law to determine its relevance for contemporary Christian faith and morality.

Two very important questions need to be asked. First, we need to ask how the Old Testament law applied in its own context and culture. Second, are there underlying theological and ethical principles that emerge from the Old Testament law that are reinforced or abrogated in the New Testament? As we will see in the New Testament, the laws against homosexuality are in fact reinforced. There are in fact principles that stand in relation to all areas of sexual conduct which are not out of date or irrelevant today.

While acknowledging this difficult area of biblical interpretation, it is nevertheless truly surprising to read certain modern students of the Bible who claim that the Old Testament law is not relevant today. They are failing to distinguish something. What they are failing to acknowledge is the distinction between major classes or kinds of Old Testament laws. There are three major kinds of law in the Law of Moses: ceremonial (or ritual or sacrificial) law, civil law and moral law. Because of their importance to this discussion, we will look at them a bit closer.

The ceremonial laws in the Old Testament have to do with the laws of sacrifice. They defined actions or events that rendered someone unclean for ceremonial purposes, such as the handling of the dead (Lev. 21:1), having any hemorrhage or emission from the body (Lev. 15), or eating of unclean food (Lev. 17:15). They are the laws that regulate the sacrificial system of the Old Testament. The people of Israel were to bring sacrifices to the altar for various kinds of sins. But these laws are fulfilled in Christ and the New Testament explicitly says that the Christian is no longer under obligation to obey them. We think of all the statements in the Book of Hebrews, for example, which say there no longer remains any sacrifice for sin. (Heb. 10:18) The writer of Hebrews is clearly setting aside the whole sacrificial system of the Old Testament because Christ has completed it. The Old Testament sacrifices were a type. Christ is the fulfillment of that type and the Christian is no longer under any obligation to make sacrifices. Here are Old Testament laws that no longer apply to us.

The civil laws have to do with the laws of punishment. They are the laws that regulate daily life in the nation of Israel such as borrowing another's livestock (Ex. 22:10-14), principles of restitution for lost property (Ex. 22:7-9), and testifying in a lawsuit (Ex. 23:1-3). Within Israel the adulterer, idolater, homosexual and the false prophet or teacher was to be punished by death. There were dietary laws that were to be obeyed, i.e., laws relating to clean and unclean foods, preparation of foods, etc. These laws had a temporary purpose and were fulfilled completely in the nation of Israel. Their temporary purpose came to an end with the death and resurrection of Christ and the pouring out of the Spirit at Pentecost and the mission of the Church into the whole world instead of just in Israel.

We can think of why these laws were temporary. In this new age of Christ and the Spirit, when the call of the Church is to go and make disciples of ALL nations, what nation would welcome Christian missionaries if they taught that adulterers or idolaters or homosexuals should be put to death? In this new age of the Spirit, these Old Testament civil laws no longer apply to God's people today. As with the ceremonial laws, they were specifically repealed in the New Testament (Mk 7:19; Eph. 2:15; Heb. 7:18; 8:13; 10:8-10). They had only a temporary life span within the nation of Israel.

The moral law has to do with the 10 Commandments. The moral law is true for all time and to be obeyed in all times and places. With regard to the Levitical law, it contains underlying principles that are universally and timelessly true. Indeed, as Gagnon points out,

"Most of Leviticus 18-20 can be thought of as an expanded commentary on the ten commandments, with prohibitions against idolatry and witchcraft, stealing and lying, adultery and incest; and commands to honor one's parents, keep the Sabbath, and to "love one's neighbor as oneself. " (Lev. 19:18)[12]

The Levitical Code, then, contains within it ceremonial, civil, and moral laws. Therefore, it would be just as wrong to say that the Christian is to obey the whole of the Levitical law as it would be to say that the whole of the Levitical law is irrelevant today. When Christians retain the moral law and live in accord with it while not following the ceremonial or civil laws, it is not that they are picking and choosing according to their own prejudices or ignorance. They do so because the New Testament in all its parts calls us to obey the moral law.

The Old Testament itself does not neatly distinguish between temporary civil and ceremonial laws and timeless moral laws. For Christians the distinction must be made on the basis of the New Testament's teaching, including its interpretations of the Old Testament. Everywhere in the New Testament there is a repetition and reapplication of the moral laws of the Law of Moses. In Romans 12 Paul summarizes most of the Ten Commandments. In the Sermon on the Mount (Matthew 5-7), Jesus reapplies parts of the Law of Moses. Throughout Paul's letters, he says you must not lie, steal, bear grudges, fornicate, etc. They are just repeating the moral laws to the Church over and over again. In contrast, the ceremonial and civil laws are never repeated.

What is reinforced in Leviticus 18:22 and 20:13— although in a negative sense—is the 6th commandment, *"You shall not commit adultery"*, which upholds the sanctity of 'one-flesh' heterosexual marriage. When you read through Leviticus 18 and 20, you find that all of the laws relating to sex serve to protect monogamous, heterosexual marriage and family. In this respect, they conform to the New Testament which also prohibits all sexual expressions that violate the integrity of heterosexual, monogamous marriage and family. Anything that undermined the sanctity of marriage—adultery, incest, bestiality, homosexuality—was prohibited and punishable in the Old Testament civil law by death. Such was the seriousness of the breaking of that God-given ordinance, the sanctity of marriage.

Leviticus 18 and 20 is a restatement, though negative, of the 'one flesh' command of Genesis which is a fundamental, divine principle that is as relevant now as it was then. Only the prohibition against having sex with a menstruating woman (reasons for which are given in Lev. 15:19-24) can be limited to an issue of distinctively Jewish ritual uncleanness. Boswell concedes that some of these prohibitions "might seem to stem from moral absolutes like incest and adultery".[13] But he still insists that the context defines them as ritual rather than moral.

I would contend, however, that the seriousness of the penalties for those things that undermine marriage—incest, homosexuality, adultery, bestiality—undermine Boswell's contention. In his commentary on Leviticus, Gordon Wenham points out that in Israel, in contrast to other near Eastern ancient law, religious offenses against life and offenses against the structure of the family were all punished more severely than anything else.[14] They were punished more severely, for example, than the crimes of theft or crimes against property. All of the laws in Leviticus 18 and 20 are in these categories: child sacrifice is a sin against both family and religion; visiting mediums is a sin against religion; the long list of sexual offenses is all sin against marriage and the family. In contrast, the surrounding nations tended to punish stealing more severely than did Israel. So theft, which Boswell calls intrinsically evil was punished less severely in Israel than incest and adultery which Boswell seems to imply may not be intrinsically evil. It is hard not to conclude from this that Boswell's moral priorities clearly conflict with the Scriptures' moral priorities.

In addition, the use of the word 'abomination' to describe homosexual intercourse cannot be limited to cultic idolatrous practices as Boswell argues. As stated above, abomination refers to something that God abhors. The Book of Proverbs uses the word many times in reference to clear moral evils, not ritual uncleanness. In Proverbs 6:16 for example, there are six things the Lord detests or hates, seven that are detestable to him: haughty eyes, a lying tongue, hands that shed innocent blood, a heart that devises wicked schemes, feet that are quick to rush into evil, a false witness that pours out lies and a man that stirs up dissention among brothers. Also in Proverbs, the Lord abhors dishonest scales and detests lying lips. Clearly, the Old Testament does not restrict the word *'to'evah'*—abomination—to things that are ritually contaminated for the Jews.

## The Historic-Biblical View

In conclusion, I would contend that the prohibitions against homosexual practice in the Leviticus Holiness Code were intended to apply to all homosexual relations. It is not the context of Canaanite and Egyptian idolatry that made homosexual practice wrong for Old Testament Jews. The Book of Leviticus teaches that homosexual acts are wrong in and of themselves because they are outside of God's created boundaries for human sexuality. They undermine marriage which God established at creation and guards by his laws. As I will attempt to point out, the New Testament builds on this teaching of the moral law.

# NINE

## New Testament Fences Around Marriage

**Romans 1:26-27**

We now turn to the New Testament passage that most students of the Bible agree is a critical text in the Bible's assessment of homosexuality, Romans 1:26-27. It is the strongest and clearest biblical passage that many believe gives us a very clear and definitive answer to the rightness or wrongness of homosexuality in general. The development of Paul's argument is very important.

> Romans 1:18 *"For the wrath of God is revealed from heaven against all ungodliness and wickedness of those who by their wickedness suppress the truth."*

> Romans 1:21 *"for although they knew God, they did not honor him as God or give thanks to him, but they became futile in their thinking, and their senseless minds were darkened."*

> Romans 1:24 *"Therefore God gave them up in the lusts of their hearts to impurity, to the degrading of their bodies among themselves."*

> Romans 1:26-27 *"For this reason God gave them up to degrading passions. Their women exchanged natural intercourse for unnatural, and in the same way also the men, giving up natural intercourse with women, were consumed with passion for one another. Men committed shameless acts with men and received in their own persons the due penalty for their error."*

Understanding the context of Paul's words is again of utmost importance. Paul's condemnation of homosexual behavior appears as an illustration of pagan immorality within a theological discussion regarding the general ungodliness of the world. Ever since the creation of the world, says Paul, all people have known of God's existence and his power by observing the natural order of what has been made and through their own moral sense (v. 32). But humankind has universally refused to acknowledge and obey this true God. It has universally refused to acknowledge that it is made in the image of God. In disregarding creation's evidence of its Maker, humankind has turned on a massive scale to idolatry.

This turning away from the true God is illustrated by reference to all homosexual behavior and all distortions of heterosexual behavior as being against nature and nature's God. They *"exchanged natural relationships for unnatural ones"*. (NIV) These homosexual acts are against the divinely created order and against God's intention for humans. Paul follows his reference to homosexuality with a long and lurid list of what he calls every kind of wickedness, greed, and depravity that flows forth from human rebellion against the Creator. In this context, then, homosexuality and distortions of heterosexuality are symptoms of the moral chaos and bankruptcy of a culture.

Paul is not arguing here that every individual, case by case, has gone through this whole process of rejecting God. For example, he is surely not saying that every homosexual person has consciously rejected God as Creator. That is simply not the case. Rather, he is making a sweeping diagnosis of the fallen human condition and its tragic consequences. Paul lists homosexuality as one evidence of God's wrath on human unrighteousness that takes the ironic form of giving people over to the lies and immoral behavior they willfully have chosen.

### New Approach and Arguments

The revisionist case is put forth powerfully by John Boswell and Robin Scroggs. The crux of Boswell's argument, which is so prominent in the current debate both outside and within the church, is that "the persons Paul condemns are manifestly not homosexual: what he derogates are homosexual acts committed by apparently hetero-sexual persons".[1] In other words, it is argued, the people Paul condemns are heterosexual people who are going against their natural inclinations (*"men and women gave up their natural and took on the unnatural"*) and engaging in homoerotic behavior. It is claimed that Paul would have had no objections to gay people, those whose natural inclina-tions are homosexual, engaging in homoerotic acts. Accord-ing to Boswell, this passage does not even have in mind gay people or homosexuals. Boswell writes, "There is no clear condemnation of homosexual acts in the verses in ques-tion".[2]

Boswell's line of reasoning is based on his contention that to Paul "nature" was not a question of universal law or truth; it did not mean a universal moral order, but rather the *personal* nature of the pagans in question.[3] Boswell believes that "against nature" signifies behavior which is unexpected, unusual or different from what would occur in the normal order of things: "beyond nature", perhaps, but not "immoral".[4] So these individual heterosexual pagans were going against, or beyond their personal heterosexual nature, and behaving in a homosexual way. They were inconsistent with their heterosexual nature by behaving homosexually. So when Paul calls homosexual relations contrary to nature, Boswell says, he did not mean they were immoral. He means rather that they are acting unexpect-edly or unusually because their sexual behavior is inconsis-tent with their heterosexual nature.

Robin Scroggs in *The New Testament and Homosexual-ity* has quite a different view of Romans. The crux of his argument is that the predominant model of homosexuality in Paul's culture was pederasty, an intrinsically exploited, temporary and unequal relationship between an adult male and a pre-adolescent boy, often a slave who had no choice in the matter.[5] When Paul thought about homosexuality, there was no other form of male homosexuality in the Greco-Roman world which could come to mind.[6] In this view, when Paul condemns homosexuality in the New Testament and even in Romans, he is not condemning homosexuality in and of itself. What Paul is condemning is the destructive qualities of pederasty. Since pederasty is so totally different from the contemporary gay-Christian model of consenting, committed, adult homosexual partnerships, the New Testament teaching doesn't apply to the current situation. It is argued that we have here an apples-and-oranges situation and not apples-and-apples. Paul's straightforward denunciation of homosexual acts in Romans 1 cannot be used in today's discussion without actually doing violence to the integrity of the New Testament itself.[7]

## Evaluating the New Arguments

There are some very serious problems in Boswell's view.

First, the men Paul describes in verse 27 are clearly not heterosexual persons performing homosexual acts as Boswell contends. It is their homosexual attraction or orientation or desire that leads to their homosexual acts. Men *"who were consumed with passion or enflamed with lust for other men"* are by definition homosexual and not heterosexual.

Second, Boswell's argument hinges on rejecting the most likely meaning of the phrase "against nature" (*para phusin*) which Paul uses in verse 26. Boswell claims that Paul means here "unexpected or unusual". He says it is people (heterosexuals) turning to unexpected, unusual relationships (homosexual), not necessarily relationships that were against nature. Boswell argues that the implication here is not that of an abrogation of a natural law or a moral order.

It is true that there are instances of both meanings of this word in the New Testament. Again, the context must determine the individual meaning of a word. In a chapter dealing with the righteousness of God and God's condemnation of the unrighteousness of fallen humanity, the implication is clearly moral. Paul puts forth a litany of rampant human lawlessness as evidence that God's wrath and judgment are already at work in the world. It is evident from the context, then, that Paul identifies 'nature' with the created order. Paul's main point in this passage is that the refusal to acknowledge God as Creator leads to a distortion

of the original creation and a distortion of sexual relationships. He uses a number of rhetorical devices, particularly
the repeated use of the verb "exchange natural for unnatural". There is a direct parallel, it seems, between the rejection of God and the rejection of created sexual roles.

In a close examination of the context of the passage, in
terms of both the logic of the argument and the rhetoric
employed, Boswell's exegesis of Romans 1:26-27 appears to
be seriously flawed and misleading. Boswell's interpretation of 'nature' as the personal nature of the individuals
involved and his claim that 'against' is best translated as
'going beyond' is untenable. The 'exchange' of natural for
unnatural is not a matter of an individual person's choice or
decision; rather it is Paul's characterization of the fallen
condition of the pagan world. Paul is treating *all* homosexual *activity* as evidence of humanity's tragic confusion
and rebellion against its Creator.

It is important also to note that this phrase "against
nature" or "contrary to nature" was a common stock phrase
used over and over again by Greco Roman moralists and
Hellenistic Jews. In the literary convention of the time, it
had the accepted meaning of contrary to nature and was
frequently used to designate homosexual acts in contrast to
heterosexual acts which were according to nature.

For example, Plutarch, whose life overlapped Paul's
life, in his dialogue on love has one of his characters dispar-
age union contrary to nature with males as contrasted to
the love between men and women which is characterized as
natural. A few sentences later this character complains that
those who consort with males willingly are guilty of weakness and effeminacy because, contrary to nature, they allow
themselves in Plato's words to be covered and mounted like
cattle. So it wasn't Paul who originated this application of
"against nature" for homosexual behavior and "natural" for
heterosexual behavior. This convention goes all the way
back at least to Plato and almost invariably the context is
that of unnatural homosexual activity being pronounced
immoral or against propriety in contrast to the natural
heterosexual relations. The categorization of homosexual
practices as *"beyond nature"* was commonplace, also, in

polemical attacks against homosexuality in the world of Hellenistic Judaism.

Hellenistic Jewish writers were particularly vehement about sexual behavior being contrary to nature. They tended to identify nature with the Law of Moses and with God's created intention. For example, Josephus, whose life overlapped Paul's as well, wrote that the Law (referring to Leviticus) recognizes no sexual connections except for the natural according to nature, the natural union of man and wife. It abhors the intercourse of males with males.[8] Paul's language and rhetoric in Romans 1 is very similar to the standard Hellenistic Jewish polemic against the Gentiles. It is clear that he too identifies nature with a universal created order with what ought to be in the world as designed by God. Those who indulge in sexual practices against nature are, therefore, defying their Creator and demonstrating their own alienation from created reality.

Philo's distaste for homosexuality is exhibited in its most elaborate expression in his telling of the Sodom story. He charges that the inhabitants of Sodom cast off the law of nature and applied themselves to drinking and forbidden forms of intercourse, and in their mad lust for women they not only violated the marriages of their neighbors but also mounted other males.[8] So there is good evidence to conclude that Paul was taking up the language of the day and using it to emphasize his point.

Richard Hays, writing in the *Journal of Religious Ethics* for spring 1986, also finds Boswell's interpretation of "against nature" untenable. But he reserves his most vigorous challenge for Boswell's claim that Paul's derogation of homosexual behavior in Romans applies only to homosexual acts committed by heterosexual persons. Hays believes Boswell's interpretation falls apart as an 'exegesis' (drawing the meaning *out of* the text) of Paul and is a textbook case of 'eisegesis,' (the fallacy of reading one's own agenda *into* a text).

Romans 1 confronts us with an account of how the ordering of human life before God has gone awry. Paul sees homosexual relations as a tragic distortion of the created order. In a brief look at the broader biblical context, Hays finds that although homosexuality is a minor concern of the biblical authors, every explicit reference is pejorative in character. Hays concludes that "in Romans 1:26-27 we find an unambiguous indictment of homosexual behavior as a violation of God's intention for humanity".[10]

There are very few critical commentaries—if any—that make the distinctions that Boswell makes. J. Wright suggests that no fewer than 22 critical 20th century commentaries on Romans that discuss this passage fail to make these distinctions of Boswell.[11] We need to ask the question he asks, "Are all these writers wrong about Romans 1? Are they all prejudiced? Have all these modern scholars overlooked and failed to notice this aspect of the verse that the history professor from Yale has discovered"? It seems that Boswell just turns a blind eye to a huge body of critical commentary on this passage. Beyond this, in spite of a number of interesting references to the early Church Fathers, Boswell seems again to have not consulted the major Patristic writings that were available at the time of his writing.

Sherwin Bailey adds to Boswell's argument the claim that Paul could not possibly have known about what we call a homosexual orientation. He writes,

> "Naturally enough, the Bible knows nothing of inversion as an inherited trait, or an inherent condition due to psychological or glandular causes, and consequently regards all homosexual practice as evidence of perversion."[12]

Homosexual orientation or 'inherent condition' was not a part of the common language of the day. Bailey draws this distinction between 'inverts' and 'perverts' and says Paul is speaking to perverts only. A pervert is a person with basically the heterosexual disposition that Boswell was describing who engages in homosexual acts.

One commentator who investigated resources to see whether or not it was known at that time if there were people who had a long term homosexual orientation found that Philo refers to those who accustom themselves to the practice of homosexual acts.[13] Josephus also indicates that homosexual behavior had become a fixed habit for some.

Clement of Alexandria in the 3rd century refers to an interpretation of Jesus' words in Matthew 19:12 concerning those who are eunuchs who have been so from birth, that some men from birth have a natural aversion to a woman and indeed those who are so constituted do well not to marry. The Bible has a clear understanding of "conditions" which are not chosen. It is likely, therefore, that Paul and his readers were not unaware of the fact that there were some people for whom homosexual intercourse was not simply a freely chosen alternative but a fixed preference or settled lifestyle. So again, Sherwin Bailey's view is very much a personal view trying to justify homosexuality.

There are others who would say that Paul is referring here only to unloving and idolatrous homosexual relationships. They would contend that he is not referring to loving, caring, responsible and gentle homosexual behavior that some Christian homosexuals practice. If it is motivated by love it is OK. Then if those with homosexual tendency want to express their love complete through physical expression, that must be right too.

But Paul's argument is so much stronger here. He argues that the whole natural order is broken. Richard Lovelace highlights this reality in these well-crafted words:

"All human sexuality, in its heterosexual as well as its homosexual forms, is disordered by the inherited drive towards disobedience which we call original sin, and by the broken social fabric of idolatrous societies. Human sin and God's punishment upon it have deeply affected the processes by which sexual identity is formed, with a result that none of us, heterosexual or homosexual, naturally desires to fulfill perfectly God's plan for our sexuality. We did not consciously choose to have the deviant's sexual orientation which drives us towards fornication, adultery, or homosexual practice. But we are confronted with the choice whether or not to act out our orientation and fulfill our natural desires, or whether instead to seek the control and transforming power of the Spirit of Christ to restrain and re-orient our desires and our behavior."[14]

Paul is most surely referring here to the outworking of homosexual behavior, not merely to motivation or disposition or to actual temptation.

Secondly, what can we say in response to Scrogg's argument? It may indeed be true that when Paul wrote of male homosexuality, pederasty was at least in the forefront of his mind since it was probably the only form of homosexuality openly practiced in the 1ˢᵗ Century Greco-Roman world. However, the fact that Paul explicitly and intentionally includes female homosexuality which was either extremely rare or practiced in secrecy indicates that he had more in mind than pederasty. This is particularly significant because Romans 1:26 is the only reference to lesbianism in the Bible. And the Greco- Roman texts are virtually silent about lesbianism. The fact that Paul departed so dramatically from the literary conventions you see him using by including lesbianism really baffles Robin Scroggs. He is puzzled that female homosexuality is mentioned at all. He asks, "Why does Paul include it here?" Then he states, "If Paul is dependent on a pre-formed tradition for these two verses, he of course found it in that tradition. Why the tradition included it is a question to which I see no answer."[15]

Scroggs is baffled because of his insistence that Paul could only have pederasty, a male phenomenon, in mind. However, if Romans 1:26-27 is a general indictment of all homosexual behavior as contrary to the created order, then the inclusion of lesbianism is totally fitting and Paul's mentioning it here is not surprising.

A serious problem with Scroggs is that he never shows from either Romans or anywhere else in Scripture that it is the pederastic element that Paul objected to in Greco-Roman homosexuality rather than the homoerotic element as such—or both. Pederasty was a very unequal relationship between men and boys. Is this what Paul is objecting to? Homosexual acts per se are between two males whether that be an equal or unequal relationship. Is this what Paul is objecting to? He is clearly objecting to the practice. But Scroggs is never able to show us from Scripture which practice Paul is objecting to. Scroggs in honesty concedes that Paul's argument from nature might mean, of course, that he might have made the same judgment about any form of homosexuality.[16] We just don't know, concludes Scroggs.

At one point in the course of Scrogg's argument, he insists that Paul's indictment of lesbian relationships as against nature has nothing to do with any theories of natural law or with interpretation of the Genesis stories of creation.[17] But at another point he says that what was most abhorrent for the Greco-Roman moralists who opposed pederasty was that it violated the natural code of creation, however creation was understood. So in one place he says Paul wouldn't have been referring to creation. In another place he says that is what the Greco-Roman moralists did and Paul was dependent upon them for what he wrote. These statements seem to contradict each other. He also tells us that the rabbinic and Hellenistic Jews used nature over and over again to refer to God's Law and the universal, normative, created order of the world as it ought to be. He goes to great length in his book to show how indebted Paul was to the language, thought forms, and rhetoric of the Greco-Roman moralists as well as the Hellenistic Jews. If that is the case, then why in Romans1 would Paul use the phrase "against nature" in a completely different way than the tradition on which he is so dependent?

It might well be the case that Scroggs misses the obvious in this passage. Paul gives homosexuality in and of itself as an illustration of the moral confusion in unrighteousness that comes when a culture refuses to acknowledge God. Richard Hays writes,

> "The illustration upon which both Paul and his readers would have regarded this particularly vivid rebellion against the Creator who may  be clearly seen in the things that have been made is made palpable in the clouding of sexual distinctions that are fundamental to God's created design."[18]

Hays is saying that the reference to God as Creator would certainly evoke, for Paul as well as for his readers, immediate recollections of the creation story in Genesis 1-2. And what does the creation story tell us? It tells us that man and woman were created for each other. The woman was taken from the man's body, bone of his bone and flesh of his flesh. She was like him when nothing else in creation was and yet not exactly like him. She was created to complement him. Thus, Paul gives a theological grounding to the created complementarity of male and female. Paul's hearers would have remembered the words of Jesus as well who referred to creation every time he talked about marriage:

> "At the beginning of creation, God made them male and female. For this reason a man shall leave his father and mother and cleave to his wife and the two will become one flesh. So they are no longer two but one. Therefore, what God has joined together, let not man separate." (Mark 10:6)

Paul and his readers also would have been aware of the radical contrast between the Genesis account and the Greek poets' accounts of the creation of the sexes. The standard belief in the Greco-Roman world was that in contrast to men, women were made of inferior material and were more like animals. Everything male was superior to anything having to do with women. There was a running debate among the writers that went back to Plato's time regarding the relative merit of same sex and opposite sex love. So, for example, Pausanius in Plato's symposium argues that noble love has no part of the female since males have the more robust nature and the larger share of mind.[19] Homosexuality was seen as superior to heterosexuality because of the female lesser mind and less robust nature. Homosexuality was more masculine. Or Protogones in Plutarch's *Erotica* says, "Genuine love has no connection whatsoever with the women's quarters. Heterosexual love is effeminate and bastard and should even be forbidden. It is devoid of manliness and friendship and inspiration."[20] For many Greek men, wives were considered necessary evils needed to produce heirs and keep house.

In wonderful and sharp contrast, the Genesis story tells of man and woman created equally in the image of God out of the same flesh and bone. The Hebrew describes the woman as a complementary equal and adequate counterpart for the man. The Hebrew word actually implies the kind of perfect fit of two ends of a belt that fit together. The amazing biological complementarity of the sexes that leads to the procreation of children is not an accident of nature. It is rather evidence of the Creator's design. Even in this running debate of the Greek pagans, procreation was one of the main arguments from nature that was used by those who believed heterosexuality was superior to homosexuality.

I think that it would be accurate and fair to say that Boswell, Bailey, Scroggs and most revisionist scholars underestimate the importance of the Bible's creation account as the backdrop and presupposition supporting all of the Bible's teaching about marriage, the family and sexuality—including Paul's reference to homosexuality in Romans 1. As Hays puts it,

> "In Romans 1, Paul portrays homosexual behavior as a sacrament so to speak, in the sense that it is an outward visible sign of an inward and spiritual reality, figuring forth through the dishonoring of their bodies."[21]

It is like a physical, visible sign of the dishonoring of their bodies. It is like a physical, visible sign of the inner spiritual condition of those who have exchanged the truth about God for a lie.

The language of exchange plays a central role in the Romans passage, emphasizing the direct parallel between the rejection of God and rejection of created sexual roles. We listen again to Paul's words:

> "Because they exchanged the truth about God for a lie and worshiped and served the creature rather than the Creator, God handed them over to the dishonoring of their bodies among themselves, their women exchanged natural relations for unnatural, the men likewise gave up natural relations with women and were consumed *with passion for one another.*" (Romans 1:26-27)

Exchanging the true God for false gods leads to an exchange of the natural for the unnatural in the visible world. It is a particularly vivid example of what Paul is trying to argue as a part of his big argument of what happens when humanity turns away from God.

In conclusion, along with the creation accounts, Romans 1 is the clearest passage in the Scriptures which answers the question of the moral rightness or wrongness of homosexual behavior. Paul establishes the intrinsic immorality of homosexual behavior irrespective of the social context, personal motivation or anything else. It is intrinsically wrong because it violates God's created sex distinction and His purposes for sexual intercourse. In the beginning, God made us male and female and called us to express sexual love within the context of heterosexual, monogamous, faithful marriage. As such, homosexual intercourse is against created human nature. As Paul reaffirms the normativity of heterosexuality, it becomes apparent that when he condemns pederasty, he not only condemns the exploitation involved in that practice, which certainly he would have hated, he also condemns the homoeroticism of men having sex with boys or with men. Paul's teaching, therefore, must be taken seriously and applied with care and sensitivity in every culture to whatever model of homosexuality may emerge.

### I Corinthians 6:9-11

The next passage that figures prominently in discussions of same-gender relationships is I Corinthians 6:9-11. In this chapter Paul is exasperated with the Corinthians, some of whom apparently had come to an exalted state of 'knowledge' with regard to their moral life. In their arrogance these Corinthian Christians had come to believe that they were beyond normal Christian moral standards. Paul confronts them with a blunt rhetorical question:

> "Do you not know that wrongdoers will not inherit the kingdom of God? Do not be *deceived! Fornicators, idolaters, adulterers*, **male prostitutes** *(malakoi)*, **sodomites** (arsenokoita), *thieves, greedy, drunkards, revilers, robbers—none of these will inherit* the kingdom of God. And this is what some of you used to be. But you were washed, you were sanctified, You were justified in the name of the Lord Jesus Christ and in *the Spirit of our God.*" I Corinthians 6:9-11 (NRSV)

Included in Paul's illustrative list of the sorts of people who will not inherit God's kingdom are persons here translated as *"male prostitutes"* and *"sodomites."*

Now in the past, people with the rather Greek view of sexual sin, i.e., seeing it as the worst of all sins, have said that anyone who shows any tendencies towards homosexuality must be a very wicked person. They have seen homosexual sin as uniquely heinous and evil and in turn have condemned and rejected from the church those who are homosexual.

What we notice immediately in this text is that Paul's list includes many other sins besides homosexuality: the greedy are mentioned alongside adulterers and thieves. Paul says that all these behaviors characterize the wicked who will not inherit the kingdom of God.

I think Paul is referring here to those who don't struggle against these sinful tendencies whatever they are. He is referring to those who don't even think that these things are wrong. I think he is talking about continuing in this lifestyle. People who continue in these behaviors and embrace them and persist in them without repentance will not inherit the kingdom of God. It seems that Paul's condemnation here is saying that these are people who are not bothering to struggle against sin at all, but are allowing it to dominate them completely. By continuing habitually in sin, it demonstrates that you really haven't understood the grace of God. This way of life, he is saying, is evidence of the unrighteousness which God cannot accept in His kingdom.

We need to look here at the meaning of the two Greek words for *"male prostitutes"* and *"sodomites"* that are translated to refer to homosexual behavior. Both of these words are ambiguous in their ancient usage and English translations through the centuries have included a wide range of meanings.

The first Greek word *"malakoi"* translated here as "male prostitute" literally means "soft". It was often used disparagingly of men who were effeminate. The Arndt-Gingrich Lexicon suggests that it refers to men and boys who allow themselves to be misused homosexually. For example, the Hellenistic Jew Philo who was a contemporary of Paul wrote a sharp condemnation of the freeborn eunuchs who dressed up as women, perfuming themselves, cropping their hair to sell their sexual favors to older men. He described their degeneracy with the noun *"malakia"*. It is the same word as *"malakoi"*. *'Malakoi'* then is best translated as the passive homosexual partner on the basis of the context, specifically the way it is put together with the second word *"arsenekoitai."*

Paul's use of *"arsenekoitai"* is the earliest known reference to this word. Even though the Greco-Roman moralists and early Church Fathers wrote at length about homosexuality, they never used this particular word. Jewish writers in later literature did use the word, however. The question here is, "What did Paul mean by it?" Here the most likely view is the one put forward by Robin Scroggs. Scroggs shows that this word *"arsenekoitai"* is a literal Greek translation of the Hebrew phrase meaning "lying with a male" which comes directly out of Leviticus 18 and 20.[22] In other words, when you look at Leviticus 20:13 in the Greek Old Testament (Septuagint), you find that there are two Greek words *"arsenos"* and *"koiten"* which mean male intercourse. It appears that Paul or some early rabbinic writer put these two words together to form the new word *"arsenekoitai"* which means sexual offender. Clearly in Leviticus the words meant homosexual practice and so clearly the Greek does as well.

If this is the origin of the word, which seems almost certain, then its absence in the writings of pagan, native-speaking Greeks who did not have contact with Jewish debate is not surprising because the word would have made little sense to them. The Church Fathers might also have aborted the word because it was an offensive, vulgar expression. They used other words for homosexuality. But it is striking here that Paul, as we know from elsewhere, did not shrink from using such a vulgar expression when making his point strongly.

*"Arsenekoitai,"* then, the Greek word translated here as "sodomite," literally means "to lie with a male". The

*"arsenekoitai"* is the male bed partner for a male in sexual intercourse. The majority of exegetes understand the words *'malakoi'* and *'arsenokoitai'* to mean the passive and active partners respectively in the male homosexual relationship.[23]

It is worthy to note that in this passage, Paul does not use any of the available common Greek words for homosexuality. He uses this new and special word that covers all types of male homosexual intercourse. He could have used *paiderastes* ("lover of boys") or *paidophthoros* ("corrupted of boys") or *arrenomanes* ("mad after males"), words that were much more specific to certain homosexual practice, but chose not to do so. Paul rather chose the most general word available.

### New Approach and Arguments

Boswell and Bailey argue that the Greek words *"malakoi"* and *"arsenekoitai"* refer to either homosexual or heterosexual male prostitutes, that is, those who are promiscuous and misuse their homosexual tendencies for their own gain.[24] They say that Paul is not referring to anyone behaving in a homosexual manner. He is not referring to those who are involved in a committed, love relationship. If it is in a loving setting, it is not wrong.

In typical style, Boswell concludes that these New Testament passages did not play a role in the development of European attitudes toward homosexuality, nor did they connote homosexuality in the time of Paul or for centuries after, nor were they determinative of Christian opinion on the morality of homosexual acts."[25] He adds that Thomas Aquinas in the 13th century was the first really influential theologian to use the passage from I Corinthians as a scriptural basis for hostility toward homosexual behavior.

Robin Scroggs argues that the pairing of these two words in Paul's vice list in I Corinthians 6:9-11 make it very likely that they refer to the younger passive partner and the older active partner in a particular kind of pederastic relationship that was universally despised in the ancient world. It would have been like a call boy, Scroggs says, a consenting effeminate youth *(malakoi)* who sells sexual favors for money and/or pleasure to an older male who would be the *'arsenekoitai'*. It is very likely that Scroggs is right here, in which case this passage refers to a specific form of homosexual prostitution. Having said that, they *need not* be so interpreted, because both words also stand well by themselves, yielding different interpretations.[26]

### Response

In summary, Paul's use of the noun *arsenokoitai* presupposes and reaffirms the Holiness Code's condemnation of homosexual acts. He asserts by including homosexual acts in his list of vices that they were formerly practiced by some of the Corinthian Christians. After coming under the Lordship of Christ, however, the believers are to leave behind these practices which they have done. *"This is what some of you used to be. But you were washed, you were sanctified, you were justified in the name of the Lord Jesus Christ and in the Spirit of our God."* In the remainder of the chapter, Paul urges the Corinthians to glorify God with their bodies because they now belong to Him and not to themselves.

### I Timothy 1:9-10

The final passage relevant to the discussion on homosexuality is I Timothy 1:9-10:

> "The law is laid down not for the innocent but for the lawless and disobedient, for the godless and sinful, for the unholy and profane, for those who kill their father or mother, for murderers, fornicators, **sodomites**, slave traders, liars, perjurers, and *whatever else is contrary to the sound teaching.*"

In this passage Paul appears to be speaking out against heretical teaching in the church. There are false teachers who are claiming to be "teachers of the law". Paul is prompted to attack this Judaistic legalism and put forth his own teaching of the law, which nonetheless affirms the restraining and normative function of the law of God.

What follows is a list of fourteen vices which include the same word *"arsenekoitai"* as was found in I Corinthians 6:9. This list, however, seems to take on a discernable structure. If one looks closely at the list, it is interesting that Paul is stressing here, almost in the order of the Commandments, the offenses against them.

- *"for the lawless and disobedient, for the godless and sinful"* (first commandment)
- *"for the unholy and profane"* (second and third commandments)
- *"for those who kill their father or mother"* (fourth commandment)
- *"for murders"* (fifth commandment)
- *"fornicators, **sodomites,**"* (sixth commandment)
- *"slave traders (kidnappers)"* (seventh commandment)
- *"liars, perjurers"* (eighth commandment)

When the law here speaks against *fornicators* and *sodomites*, that is, against both heterosexuals and homosexuals, it is a negative way of reinforcing the 6th Commandment, *"You shall not commit adultery,"* in that both engage in sexual intercourse outside the one flesh marriage covenant which the commandment upholds. It is once again clear that Paul's strong words apply to homosexual *behavior*. The issue of disposition, or temptation, is not being considered here.

### New Approach and Arguments

Scroggs draws attention to the two Greek words that come immediately before and after *"arsenekoitai"*. The word immediately preceding it, translated "fornicators," is the Greek word *"pornos"*. Scroggs argues, however, that *"pornos"* could effectively function in relationship to "arsenekoitai" in the same way as *"malakos"* does in I Corinthians which would give it the narrower meaning of "male prostitute." He believes his argument is further supported by the third word *"andropodistes"* here translated "slave traders" or "kidnappers". In the culture of the day, a person was kidnapped normally only to be sold into slavery. When Scroggs puts the three words together they are translated: "male prostitutes, males who lie [with them], and slave dealers [who procure them]". He argues that with this possible translation the door is opened to ask whether Paul's earlier reference to the law is to civil law or moral law.

While "*pornos*" in classical literature can mean "male prostitute," it usually is taken by New Testament scholars to refer to sexual crimes in general, thus translated here "fornicators" or "immoral persons". (RSV) This translation is strengthened when one sees that the context is one of moral law. What seems apparent to so many is that the vice list is drawn from the 10 Commandments. This would mean that Paul's earlier reference to law is indeed the moral law. Within the context of this inherent, universal moral law, "sodomites" would not be limited only to whatever particular model of homosexuality Paul may have had in mind, but to homosexuality in general.

However, with Scroggs' undying commitment that Paul must have had - indeed could only have had - pederasty in mind, he concludes,

"The vice list in I Timothy is not condemnatory of homosexuality in general, not even pederasty in general, but that specific form of pederasty which consisted of the enslaving of boys or youths for sexual purposes, and the use of these boys by adult males."[27]

### Response

Given the ambiguities of the two critical words in I Corinthians 6:9-10, this text alone may not settle the argument about the morality of homosexuality in general. However, the I Timothy 1:9-10 passage may be weightier in the current debate than might first appear to be the case. The vice list drawn from the moral law, the 10 Commandments, puts the reference to "sodomites" into a wider moral context than whatever particular form of homosexuality may have been prevalent or in Paul's mind at the time. The protective boundary of the sixth commandment placed around the original creation ordinance of marriage prohibits any and all forms of sexual immorality, including homosexual behavior, *irrespective of* the quality of the relationship.

But what we must not miss is the tremendous hope that the I Corinthians 6 passage gives. We note the past tense in this Corinthian text. The Christians Paul was addressing had indeed been involved in all of the sins he mentions, including homosexuality. But there was the possibility of forgiveness and new life. Some of the Christians in Corinth had been practicing homosexuals and by God's grace they were no longer. They had been washed and sanctified and justified. Paul is saying that the experience of baptism can change people even with reference to their sexual behavior. In and through Christ, these Christians in Corinth had come to know the reality of freedom from guilt and holiness of life that can follow. The same hope is true of the experience of many today and is a hope for many others.

What can we conclude from having looked at the biblical passages that bear upon the discussion of homosexual acts? First, we understand that all of us to some extent are sexual deviants with aberrations of fantasy and behavior. There is not one of us who is the perfect sexual being that God intended us to be when He made us male and female. We are all broken and fallen.

Second, we understand that the norm for sexuality is heterosexuality which is firmly rooted in the Scriptural teaching on creation and then reinforced over and over again by the negative condemnations of homosexual behavior. Like extreme expressions of anger, homosexual tendencies are the result of the brokenness of our fallen world and human nature. Homosexual practice represents a move *away* from the one flesh ideal that God intends for the most intimate of human relationships. Heterosexuality represents a move *toward* the one flesh ideal God intended. So if you allow your homosexual orientation to govern your lifestyle, your behavior is moving you away from God's ideal. If you allow your heterosexuality to govern your lifestyle within the right context, your behavior is moving you toward God's ideal.

Third, we understand that sexual sin basically is not worse than other sins. We must resist the temptation to think or see it as the most terrible. Obviously, homosexual sin does involve other people and therefore it can and most assuredly does produce worse consequences but before God, sins such as pride and jealousy are just as bad.

By way of summary, in this section we have been concerned with answering the Christian Church's first major question, "Is homosexual behavior contrary to the will of God?" Together, we have endeavored to make a reasoned, theological reflection by undertaking a careful biblical exegesis of the relevant biblical passages. We have looked carefully and in some depth at the new interpretations of these same texts. We have followed and considered their arguments carefully to see if their interpretations merit acceptance. My reasoned conclusion is that the revisionist view, although well meaning and compassionate, remains an unacceptable and untenable attempt to frame theology in light of experience—in many ways ingenious and convenient, but not convincing. We cannot, therefore, condone homosexual behavior. We answer the first question in the affirmative. We find homosexual acts to be sinful. We find homosexual behavior to be contrary to the will of God and God's purpose and desire for human beings.

# TEN
## Analogy Arguments

### Gentile Inclusion Analogy

In the current debate on homosexuality, certain analogies are drawn on repeatedly in arguing against the Bible's long-standing condemnation of homosexual practice. Since they play such an influential role in the debate, it is important that we at least briefly look at their use and credibility. There are four that are most common. The first is the Gentile inclusion analogue.

In Acts 15 we read where the early Church struggled with this issue of Gentile inclusion. It is argued that the early Church initially did not think that Gentiles were to be recipients of the Gospel message, at least not apart from full observance of the Mosaic Law. However, there were faithful followers of Christ who followed Jesus' example of seeking out those excluded by law and custom. These followers carried on Jesus' work, most notably in the heroic struggle to include the Gentiles without requiring that they first become circumcised Jews. It is claimed that this heroic struggle prevailed and in effect, God made another standard, shattering what was previously understood as required for God's people.

In like manner, it is argued, the Church today does not view homosexual persons as fellow members of the body of Christ in the same way as it views other members of the body. By not affirming same-sex unions and not allowing practicing homosexuals to serve as pastors in the Church, the Church is alienating and excluding these persons from full participation and fellowship. The Church needs to look at the inclusion of the Gentiles in the early Church as a precedent to follow. Just as God's Spirit did a new thing in that day, so God's Spirit is doing a new thing in the Church today. God is shattering what was previously understood by God's people and setting a new standard. Just as the Church came to accept Gentiles into the Church without requiring that they first become circumcised, so today homosexual persons should not have to become something else first before being affirmed in the church.

As Robert Gagnon points out, the main problem with this analogy is that it involves a series of category confusions.[1] Ethnic identity which is an immutable condition of heredity is confused with homosexual self-definition which is mutable and not directly heritable. Being a Gentile which is only incidentally linked to sinful behavior is confused with being homosexual which is directly linked to sinful behavior. Including Gentiles in the Church without requiring them to be circumcised, as was required of Jews, is confused with homosexual acts which are negative moral acts forbidden for Jews and Gentiles alike. Inclusion of Gentiles which has to do with welcoming people is confused with accepting the behavior of homosexual people. Expanding salvation for uncircumcised Gentiles which has some Old Testament precedent is confused with a positive assessment of same-sex intercourse which has no precedent in Scripture. Inclusion of uncircumcised Gentiles which has uniform New Testament approval is confused with acceptance of homosexual practice which has uniform New Testament disapproval.

An analogy by definition assumes that if things have some similar attributes, their other attributes will be similar. The dissimilarities of these two things and the massive category confusions that are involved between them make the attempt at analogy between Gentile inclusion and the acceptance of same-sex unions highly unconvincing.

But what really took place in Acts 15 and what does the inclusion of the Gentiles actually entail? When the Holy Spirit was poured out upon the Gentiles, these first Jewish Christians did not immediately conclude from that experience that their Scriptures were mistaken to have spoken of the election of Israel. On the contrary, this experience compelled them to reread those Scriptures in which they discovered something they had previously overlooked: that God's special love for Israel was grounded not in nature but in His covenant and commitment; that from the beginning, God's covenant with Abraham was intended for the blessings of all nations, so that the Gentiles too might come to Zion.

What did the inclusion of the Gentiles actually entail? Paula Fredriksen has summarized it briefly and concisely.[2] The Jews of Jesus' time were quite ready to deal with interested Gentiles on several different bases. Many Gentiles, while continuing to worship their ancestral gods, added worship of Israel's God and adopted as much or as little of Jewish practice as they wished. With that Jews had no quarrel. If, however, a Gentile actually wanted to convert to Judaism, he had to give up the worship of his ancestral deities and observe Torah (e.g., its requirement of circumcision for men, its dietary restrictions, its Sabbath observance). So the Gentile either had to remain a kind of "fellow traveler," an interested outsider, or become a Jew. When, however, the Spirit was poured out upon the Gentiles, the Church did a new thing: Gentiles were to give up their pagan gods and worship the God of Israel alone, yet this did not mean that they had to become Jews (by being circumcised, keeping the Sabbath, etc.). To turn to Israel's God did mean, however, to seek holiness of life. To renounce their ancestral gods meant renouncing behavior associated with idolatrous rejection of God's creative design for human life—behavior that on the evidence of Romans 1 includes homosexual behavior. That is what the inclusion of the Gentiles actually meant.

When those first Jewish Christians saw what seemed to be the Holy Spirit being poured out upon the Gentiles, they did not regard that experience as self-authenticating. Human experience never is. They turned back to their Scriptures to try to make sense of the experience. In their rereading of those Scriptures, the Holy Spirit opened their eyes to see what they had not understood before. From the beginning, God's covenant with Abraham was meant for the blessing of all nations. To argue that the inclusion of the

Gentiles is a ground for inclusion of same-sex couples within the Church, one would need a similar reading of Scripture. It is not sufficient to make the claim that the Scriptures are wrong and simply appeal to experience and claim that this experience is the work of the Spirit.

The inclusion of the Gentiles is a poor and confusing precedent to use in arguing for the affirming and sanctioning of same-sex unions in the Church.

### Slavery Analogy Argument

A second common analogy used to argue against holding firm to the Church's long- standing condemnation of same-sex behavior is slavery. It is argued that the Church held for many centuries that slavery was an acceptable practice with good biblical support. In the 19th and 20th Centuries Christians struggled with and finally rejected the Bible's condoning of slavery. The Church set aside the scriptural mandate and precedent of slavery at that time and therefore should be open to setting aside the scriptural mandate and precedent of condemning homosexual practice as well.

There are good reasons why the analogue of slavery is a poor argument. First, the allegation that there is a scriptural mandate for slavery is simply not true. To be sure both the Old and New Testaments speak of and describe the practice of slavery in the societies of their day. In the Old Testament, Israelite law put various restrictions on enslaving fellow Israelites - the right of near-kin redemption, treating slaves as hired laborers and not as slaves, mandatory release dates, run-away slaves were not to be returned to their masters. In the Old Testament times there were these laws that regulated the practice of slavery.

In the New Testament, Paul regarded freedom from slavery as a good thing. The most important reality in life, he says, is being released from the bondage of sin and experiencing the freedom there is in Christ. Even a slave can know and experience this freedom. If in addition to gaining this spiritual freedom, however, a slave can also obtain freedom from social slavery, that is all the better. For then one can live a life of freely serving others as a slave of Christ.

Nowhere does Scripture command or encourage or sanction slavery. There is no enforcement of slavery in Scripture the transgression of which would incur a penalty. Rather, the Scriptures regulate existing situations. The Bible's teaching is always in the direction of the curtailment and eradication of slavery. In sharp contrast, there are specific commands in Scripture that forbid homosexual behavior. Nowhere in Scripture is same-sex intercourse encouraged or sanctioned. It is precisely the opposite. All the references to homosexuality without exception are negative and condemnatory.

Simply put, in Scripture slavery and homosexuality are not similar phenomena. Therefore, it is not only confusing but straightforwardly misleading to speak of both slavery and homosexual practice as mandates and precedents in the Scripture.

Secondly, the prohibitions against same-sex intercourse in the Scriptures are fences that protect the heterosexual norm of marriage established at creation. They are rooted back in the God-ordained structures of creation that were established prior to the fall of man into sin. The practice of slavery is very different. It is a post-Fall reality that has risen in a broken, sinful world and is not grounded in any pre-Fall structures. Again, the two phenomena are on such different footing in Scripture that there is no honest justification for using one to establish the other. Robert Gagnon summarizes it well when he says,

> "It is time to recognize that slavery is really quite a silly analogue to choose, one that reflects poorly on the hermeneutical acumen of those who apply it to the issue of same-sex intercourse."[3]

### Divorce/Remarriage Analogy

A third common analogy used in argument against the Church's current position on same-sex relationships is that of divorce and remarriage. In the past the church has been very reluctant to tolerate divorce. When a divorced person sought remarriage, the pastor's inquiry most often had to do with the 'guilt' or 'innocence' of the person in accordance with Jesus' allowance of remarriage following divorce if one is the victim of an unfaithful spouse. It is noted that in recent years the church has moved in the direction of practicing a more open view on divorce and remarriage. It is argued that the change to a more open view serves as a precedent for changing our views on homosexuality.

This analogy warrants a closer look at the Bible's teaching on divorce and remarriage. And because this subject is one of the more pressing issues of the day, I'll spend a little more time on it.

In the Old Testament we do not learn a great deal about divorce and remarriage. We are told that God hates divorce. (Malachi 2:16) Beyond this we learn that divorce happens. People are fallen sinners. We learn that the grounds of divorce were wider than adultery. (Deut. 24:1-4) Divorce was not approved of. It was not commanded, encouraged, sanctioned or condoned. Rather, it was tolerated and regulated (most likely to protect the rights of the divorced woman) while always seen as an evil. The right of remarriage was simply assumed. It was simply assumed that the woman, having been divorced by the first husband, would marry a second husband. There was no disapproval of this remarriage given.

In the New Testament Jesus strongly condemns the whole practice of divorce. (Matthew 19:6b) He calls his hearers back to the sanctity and permanence of marriage. But then he gives the one proper ground for divorce— marital unfaithfulness. In doing so Jesus changes the Old Testament Mosaic practice in two ways. In one way he makes divorce less strict because he lessens the penalty (i.e. death) for adultery. But in another way he makes it stricter by limiting the grounds of divorce to adultery or marital unfaithfulness. Where Jesus permits divorce, I believe he permits remarriage. Jesus says *"whoever divorces his wife, except for marital unfaithfulness, and marries another commits adultery"*. (Matthew 19:9) It seems to me it is a matter of simple logic that he would be saying that any one who divorces his wife <u>for</u> marital unfaithfulness and marries another <u>does not</u> commit adultery.

In I Corinthians 7:10-16 Paul begins by summarizing all that Jesus had to say about divorce. As with Jesus he recognizes that divorce is wrong but it happens. Then Paul turns to the matter of religiously mixed marriages and gives a second ground for divorce. In the case of a Christian being married to a non-Christian, if the non-Christian spouse refuses to remain in the marriage Paul says the believer is to let the unbeliever go. Paul says *"in such a case the brother or sister is not bound"*. (v. 15) In such a situation, I understand Paul to be saying that the brother or sister is free to remarry—otherwise they are very much bound.

The following points and extended comments are made by way of summarizing the Scripture's teaching on divorce and remarriage:

- Divorce is never commanded or even encouraged. Even in the case of marital unfaithfulness, forgiveness and reconciliation is always the better way. Divorce is always failure.

- There are two situations where divorce is not good but permitted: marital unfaithfulness and desertion by an unbelieving spouse.

- Where proper ground exists, remarriage is proper because the first marriage has been truly dissolved.

- Where there has been a divorce for insufficient reasons, remarriage is prohibited and yet that prohibition is not punitive. Its purpose is to hold the door open for reconciliation.

- There may be those times when divorce without remarriage is the least of two evils, the best one can achieve in the midst of a sinful and broken world.

In light of the Bible's teaching, when the argument is made that the more open view on divorce and remarriage is a precedent for changing our views on homosexuality, the question must be asked in all seriousness, "Is this more open view a good precedent to follow?" In light of Scripture, might it be that we ought to challenge the precedent? If the Church has been unfaithful in upholding the teaching of Jesus and Scripture on divorce and remarriage, then instead of that precedent being used to justify changing our view on homosexuality, the precedent itself is the thing that needs to undergo change.

Even within this more open view of divorce and remarriage, divorce is seen by the Church as a mark of the sinful failure of those involved. It is something that needs God's forgiveness for the part one has played in the failure of the marriage. God hates divorce. Adultery is a terrible sin. We read what the Old Testament says about it. Yet, it is not the unforgivable sin. God doesn't treat it that way. There is forgiveness even for the repentant one who has committed adultery. And I find nothing in Scripture that would indicate that the repentant adulterer may not remarry. But we name sin as sin and we call for repentance and extend God's forgiveness and encourage the forgiven sinner to move on and sin no more. He is called not to perpetuate a cycle of divorce and remarriage. While recognizing that it does happen, the Church does not and ought never to celebrate divorce.

In contrast, advocates of same-sex relationships affirm homosexual unions and ask us to celebrate these unions as expressions of legitimate, alternative sexual behavior. Their view is that the ongoing homosexual practices within these relationships are not sinful. Therefore, there is no need for repentance for sin or forgiveness of sins. Homosexual advocates are asking the church to condone behavior that Scripture clearly and unequivocally identifies as sin. The consequences of living in a persistent attitude of unrepentance and rebellion could not be more serious. A rebellious heart which steadfastly persists in unrepentant sin separates one from God. Yet, homosexual sin is not the unforgivable sin. There is forgiveness for the repentant one who has committed same-sex acts. But we name sin as sin and call for repentance and extend God's forgiveness and encourage the forgiven sinner to move on and sin no more. The Church ought never to celebrate sinful acts.

Is the divorce and remarriage analogy a good analogy in arguing for acceptance of homosexuality? The failure of the church to uphold Jesus' and the Scriptures' teaching on divorce and remarriage is a poor precedent to use. And as far as the repeatable and unrepentant nature of sin involved in homosexual practice goes, the two situations are worlds apart.

## Women in Ministry

The ordination of women is also used as a precedent in arguing for accepting committed same-sex unions in the Church. It was the traditional practice of the Church for centuries not to allow women into leadership positions in the Church. That traditional practice in our day has been re-evaluated and a number of major church bodies now ordain women for ministry. The argument is put forward that as the Church changed its view and practice of women in ministry so it should also change its view and accept committed homosexual unions in the Church.

This analogy too is a weak one for obvious reasons. First, a woman behaving as a woman is not a sin. Being a woman is an innate genetic condition given in the womb. No matter how opposed one might have been to ordaining women in ministry, no clearheaded person ever argued that women should not be ordained because behaving as a woman was a sin. In addition, a woman's erotic desire for a man is good and natural and not in and of itself linked to sinful behavior. In contrast, homosexuality is a behavioral and mental condition, neither biological nor exclusively psychological, but a mixture of many factors. The homosexual condition is a mutable condition which can be heightened or reduced and sometimes even eliminated. Moreover, erotic desire for a person of the same sex is in and of itself directly linked to sinful behavior.

Second, the arguments for ordaining women may have rightly reasoned that the historic case for not ordaining women was not solidly based on biblical teaching. It may also have rightly reasoned that the biblical teaching on the question is not completely clear and consistent.[4] On that basis it changed its view and began the practice of ordaining women. Ordination, much less ordination of women, of course, was not a question for the early Church. But does the Bible know anything of women in leadership positions? In the Old Testament there are positive precedents for putting women in leadership roles in such persons as Miriam, Deborah, Huldah and Esther. In the New Testament we have the examples of the women involved in the ministry of Jesus and Priscilla and other women who served as co-workers with Paul. There are positive precedents. In addition, Paul's admonition that *"women should be silent in the churches"* (I Corinthians 14:34) needs to be balanced by elsewhere women being allowed to pray and prophesy in the Church. (I Corinthians 11:5)

For the ordination of women to serve as a good precedent for the Church changing its current position on homosexual unions, one would need to show that the historic position on homosexuality is not solidly based on biblical teaching and identify precedents for homosexual behavior in the Bible. It would also have to show that the biblical teaching on the question of homosexual behavior is not completely clear and consistent. No such precedents for homosexual behavior are found anywhere in the Bible. Moreover, the Biblical teaching on the question of homosexual unions is uniformly consistent throughout both the Old and New Testaments in its condemnation of homosexual behavior.

Thirdly, Paul's statement that in Christ Jesus *"there is neither male nor female"* (Galatians 3:28) has been taken by some homosexual advocates in an essentially monistic way. The claim is made that Paul is doing away here with all distinctions between male and female, between heterosexual and homosexual orientations, between good and bad forms of sexual behaviors. Male and female, heterosexual and homosexual orientation, heterosexual and homosexual behavior—all these contradictions and distinctions have been overcome and are one in Christ. The context of the verse, however, will not permit that sort of reading. Paul's statement here is not sociological but redemptive. Paul is talking about salvation in this passage. When it comes to being justified by faith in Jesus Christ we have all been baptized into Christ. There is only one salvation for the Jew and the Greek, for the slave and the free, for the male and the female. When it comes to salvation in Christ, there are no differences. This verse does not in any way speak of obliterating sexual differences and accepting same-sex unions in the Church.

The analogy of the ordination of women is simply a poor analogy.

**Part 3**

# What is to be the Church's Attitude?

# ELEVEN
## Attitudes and Understanding

In this final section, we respond to the second major question facing the Christian Church: "What is to be the Church's attitude toward homosexuals?" The answer to this question too is of crucial importance. Based on the understanding gained in Part 1 and on the exegesis and theological reflection set forth in Part 2, what is to be the Christian's attitude toward those struggling with homosexual temptation?

***The attitude of repentance.*** Maybe up to this time the Church's starting point has been wrong. Christians have tended to start with 'them' instead of 'us'. As such the attitudes of our hearts have not been right. Repentance involves change, a change of mind and heart. I believe that the way forward needs to begin with the Church repenting of its attitudes of rejection and scorn of homosexual persons. We in the church need to acknowledge and confess on behalf of ourselves and others our history of hateful and prejudicial treatment of gay and lesbian persons. We must confess that under the guise of righteousness, the church has shown little of the love and compassion of Jesus Christ. Jesus' attitude and treatment of the woman at the well (John 4:4-26) and the woman caught in adultery (John 8:3-11) has not characterized our attitude and treatment of homosexual persons.

In his very helpful book, *Homosexuality: What Should Christians Do About It?*, Richard Lovelace sets forth a prescription for a healthy church life in which Christian homophiles can be fully welcomed members. He concludes that there is need for a 'double repentance': a repentance by the homosexual person whom God calls to forego homosexual practices and draw on the grace and power of the Spirit of God for holy living, and by the 'straight' members of the church to forego pride, prejudice, hostility and homophobia. Lovelace writes:

"Persons who are compulsively uneasy, fearful, or filled with hatred when relating to persons involved in sexual sin, either homosexual or heterosexual, need a releasing work of the Holy Spirit, freeing their own sexual natures, building in them a sense of security which will permit them to express Christian love while standing firm against impurity."[1] I would commend the place to start is with a repentant heart.

***The attitude of humility.*** The bible, I hope I have shown, clearly teaches that homosexual behavior is sinful. But the bible does not teach that it is the worst of sins. Nor does it teach that homosexual sins set people apart as though they are sub-human, some kind of moral monsters who are different from all other sinners. In fact, there is no Hebrew or Greek word for a homosexual person as such. Scripture simply does not identify people by their sexual orientation as our culture does now. It does not identify any of us by our besetting temptations or sins. Rather, all of the bible's references to homosexuality specify homosexual behavior or acts. Beyond that, every biblical reference to homosexual sin occurs in passages which include a list of other sins. These lists include sexual sins which are heterosexual in nature but also sins of idolatry, greed, disobedience to parents, pride, injustice to the poor, drunkenness, slander, self-indulgence, gossip, and murder. It is scandalous when heterosexual Christians rant and rave against homosexuality as a detestable abomination to God while excusing themselves of other sins that the bible calls abominations, like lying, gossip, stirring up dissention, dishonest business practices and self-righteousness. The Book of Proverbs (see Prov. 6:16-19) tells us very clearly that these things also are detestable to God. When one watches Jesus carefully, one notices that he dealt with sins of the flesh far more leniently than he did sins of the spirit.

We need to remember, then, that we *all* sin and that none of us can look down upon another. In the sexual area, for example, we are all sexual deviants to some degree. Is there any one of us who has not had a lustful thought that has deviated from God's perfect ideal of sexuality? Nobody save Jesus Christ has been sexually sinless. We must never forget the powerful impact of Paul's rhetorical reversal in Romans 2:1: all of us stand *"without excuse"* before God, Jews and Gentiles alike, heterosexuals and homosexuals alike. There are no grounds for self-righteous condemnation of homosexual behavior. We do not have a Greek view of sin. Homosexual sin is not the worst sin in the book! Jesus said it would *"be more tolerable . . . for Sodom at the judgment than for communities* (that were probably respectable) *which reject his word and his workers"*. (Luke 10:12) Jesus does identify Sodom and Gomorrah with sin. But he argues that the sins of Sodom and Gomorrah are no worse than the sins of people who disregarded his claims and yet who probably outwardly were respectable. In Jesus' eyes the sins of pride and hypocrisy are worse than sexual sins. All of us stand under the judgment of God and are in urgent need of the grace and forgiveness of God.

***Attitude of love.*** Jesus says the whole law is summed up in the two great commandments: to love God and to love our neighbor as ourselves. Loving your neighbor as yourself involves the imaginative work of putting ourselves in the shoes of our neighbor, including our homosexual neighbor, and thinking and feeling what they are thinking and feeling. Loving your neighbor as yourself means showing hospitality to the stranger, that is, the one who is not like me, particularly the needy. God's Word does not say welcome people into your home except, of course, homosexuals. Loving your neighbor as yourself means having compassion on those who have been afflicted with AIDS and other serious health problems because of a homosexual lifestyle. The homosexual person is my neighbor and I am to love him as myself.

Christian love shows itself in associating with sexually immoral non-Christians. On one occasion, Paul rebukes the Corinthian Christians for refusing to associate with immoral persons outside the church. In I Corinthians 5:9-10, he strongly rebukes the Christians because they withdrew from contact with sexually immoral non-Christians. He says, "You must not do that. You would have to withdraw from the world to do that." Paul knows that we were not meant to withdraw from the world but to be involved in the world as salt and light.

Love shows itself also in the way we talk about people. Gay bashing and joking is cruel and sinful. Do we understand the kind of affect the terms "queer," or "queenie," or "faggot," or "pervert," have on a gay person? When a male refers to another male using those nicknames, he is hurling the most hurtful labels imaginable at that man. Those words devastate as they cut deep into a person's spirit. No ethnic label hurts as much. No IQ reference hurts a man as much. No label wreaks more havoc in the heart of a man than those words directly associated with the subject of homosexuality. The telling of gay jokes has the same effect. They are devastating. They kill and destroy.

In his epistle, James writes that one cannot praise God and with the same tongue curse men and women who are made in God's likeness. If we curse others, our praise of God becomes suspect. We need always to be asking ourselves about how we talk about homosexuality in our churches, in our families, at work, at school, with friends. Do we talk in such a way that it would be impossible for a church member, family member, relative or friend to confide in us if they struggle with homosexual temptation? We must show Christian humility and love toward all our fellow human beings. That includes gays and lesbians.

Bell Hooks is a black feminist, social thinker, memoirist and teacher. She is pro-lesbian. In one of her writings, she talks about a black woman pastor:

"In the past year, I talked with a black woman Baptist minister who although concerned about feminist issues, expressed very negative attitudes about homosexuality because, she explained, the

Bible teaches that it is wrong. Yet, in her daily life, she is tremendously supporting and caring of gay friends. When I asked her to explain this contradiction, she argued that it was not a contradiction, that the Bible also teaches her to identify with those who are exploited and oppressed and to demand that they be treated justly. To her way of thinking, committing a sin did not mean that one should be exploited or oppressed."[2]

This black woman Baptist pastor strikes me as one who is really trying to make a separation between what Christians always talk about—loving the sinner and hating the sin; loving people without condoning sin. Bell Hooks goes on and condemns this woman for her homophobia because her approach and practice isn't good enough. Hooks won't clear her of the accusation of homophobia until she can embrace homosexuality as right and say that lesbianism is fine. But here is a good example of what the Christian needs to be striving for. We need to strive to love the sinner while hating the sin, for Jesus commands us to love our neighbor as ourselves. We are to love the neighbor even though in so doing, we will be accused of being homophobic by many people.

***Attitude of acceptance.*** We are also called to accept one another as God has accepted us. How has God accepted us? God has loved and accepted us with all our hang-ups, dispositions, experiences and histories. God has loved and accepted us with all our warts and shortcomings and failures. He has loved and accepted us with all our distortions and perverted tendencies to irrational anger, jealousy, pride, and heterosexual and homosexual tendencies. This is the heart of the Gospel. He does not tell us that we have to pick ourselves up, clean ourselves off and make ourselves worthy before coming to him. We are invited simply to open up our eyes to his love and forgiveness. We are invited to come just as we are. And oh how desperately we need someone to love and accept us as we are! This is exactly what God does. He loves and accepts us with all our anger and jealousy and pride and sexual tendencies. He loves and accepts us while not necessarily approving of the outworking of those tendencies.

Jesus demonstrated this attitude of love and acceptance one day while sitting at a well with a woman of Samaria. (John 4:4-26) The woman had been married five times. Jesus never approved of her multiple marriages, but he didn't allow them to disqualify her from receiving Living Water from him. He accepted her. He accepted her without approving of her behavior. And this woman's life was drastically changed when she realized she was accepted. Jesus shows us there is a huge difference between accepting and approving. We are to be as accepting of others as Jesus was accepting of the Samaritan woman. We are to be as accepting of others as God has been accepting of us. But this 'acceptance' means that he fully and freely forgives all who repent and believe. It is not that he condones our continuance in sin. We are to accept one another as fellow-penitents and fellow-pilgrims, not as fellow-sinners who are resolved to persist in our sinning. No acceptance by God or church is promised to us if we persistently stiffen our hearts against God's Word and will. If we harden our hearts there is only judgment.

As with the Samaritan woman, the evidence that we have accepted Christ's love for us is a changed life. It is the love of Christ that compels us no longer to live for ourselves, but for him who died and was raised for us. (II Corinthians 5:15) His way is often hard but it is the only way of true joy. It is a way we cannot walk in our own strength, but we have the promise of the help of the Holy Spirit. One day in the future the struggle will be over and our joy will be complete. But until then, with the help of God's Spirit and patience in suffering, we can be more than conquerors. (Romans 8:37) The homosexual person who may not be relieved entirely of his *condition* will nevertheless always have the power of God's Spirit to draw upon to control his *behavior*.

***Attitude of compassion.*** There is the story in the New Testament of a man traveling from Jerusalem to Jericho who fell victim to robbers who stripped him and beat and left him for dead. A couple of religious people of that day came upon him lying along the road but they passed him on the other side. But then a man from Samaria came along and this man, the story says, saw him and had compassion on him. He tended to his wounds and took him to an inn.

Have you ever wondered what went through the mind of this robbed and beaten Jew when he woke up the next day in a clean bed, all bandaged up, room and board paid for by someone else? I'll bet, when he came to and looked around that room and realized that someone was covering the tab, he said to himself, "Who did this? What motivated whoever it was to take care of me? Why didn't he turn away like everybody else? Whoever it was, what made this person who bandaged me up and brought me here different?"

Jesus' story was an indictment both of the religious establishment of his day and that of any day in which the church is not reaching out in compassion to meet the needs of the neighbor. It is an indictment against any church that has become so unlike Christ who, although he always held firmly to the Truth, did so with such grace and whose life and ministry was marked not by dismay in the midst of a very evil world but was marked by compassion. When Jesus came to the city of Nain and saw in a funeral procession a dead man, the only son of a mother who was a widow, being carried out of the city, we are told that Jesus was moved with compassion for this heartbroken woman. He reached out to the coffin and raised the young man from the dead. (Luke 7:11-15) On another occasion Jesus saw the needs of the crowd around him and was moved with compassion. He proceeded to teach them and feed them. (Mark 6:30-44) Yet again, a leper comes to Jesus and falls before him saying, *"If you will, you can make me clean,"* and we read that Jesus was moved by the need of this leper. He stretched out his hand to this man that no one else would touch and healed him of his leprosy. (Mark 1:40-42) We notice that in each of these instances Jesus was moved with compassion, that is, he not only had pity for, but he *did* something to meet human need. In this non-compassionate world, the Christian is called to have Christ's attitude of compassion for the neighbor's need.

Someone has said that homosexuals are the lepers of modern society. Who is reaching out and touching them? I think here of a woman in our congregation who meets with me for support once a month and whom I admire very much. She volunteers to be with people who, in their last stages of life, are dying because of AIDS. In hospice care she goes into their homes, tends to their physical and medical needs, ministers to them spiritually as opportunity presents itself, and walks with them until they die. In the last 25 years, she has walked the last weeks of life with close to 360 persons. The large majority (80-85%) of these men and women have contracted HIV through homosexual activity. She sees their needs and doesn't shrink back, but has compassion on them. She is different. Her love for Christ has made her different. I see Christ's attitude in her as she reaches out compassionately to those who others don't want to touch. We all are to have this mind which is in Christ Jesus.

# TWELVE

## Communities of Grace

The sexual revolution of the 1970s has left society wounded and damaged with regard to sexuality. It has destabilized marriage. Some are seriously wondering if the traditional family is dying out in the West, the unit that has historically been the bedrock institution and shock absorber of society. The sexual revolution has fostered promiscuity. Forty percent of ninth graders in America have had sexual intercourse, many with multiple partners. It has been a factor contributing to the suicide rate among American teenagers tripling during the last thirty years. Millions of people have been destroyed emotionally and psychologically. It has been a contributing factor to our children learning about their sexuality by watching pornography on the internet. It is estimated that one-third of all internet users view pornography.[1] And now more recently the gay rights movement has grown up within this milieu of sexual chaos and is leaving a trail of broken lives in its wake. This throwing off of sexual limits and restraints has left people confused and concerned for the well being of children, families and society.

### Addressing the Issue Within the Church

In the midst of this confusion and moral relativism, the church has a responsibility to be salt and light in society. We cannot just sit by and dispassionately watch people destroy their lives! It is imperative that the Church of Jesus Christ speak a word of hope and clarity into the present situation. Love compels us to speak a life-giving Word of forgiveness, provide safe places of healing, as well as speak the biblical limits God has set for the expression of our sexuality.

Local churches must have the nerve and courage to speak to the issues of sexuality in our society. The Lordship of Christ over *all* of life compels us to do so. The command of Christ to love our neighbor calls forth an obedience. If we are not willing to address controversial issues, can we but conclude that our Christianity has become anemic and weak and suffered a loss of nerve? It is crucial that we address matters of human sexuality. It is crucial that we relate to the gay and lesbian people in our midst. They are not going away. They are here to stay. Increasingly, our people are interacting with gays and lesbians in their families, friendships, neighborhoods, schools, work places, and community. They are in our churches. To ignore their needs and pain is not only unloving but wrong.

The place to begin is with understanding. Our people need to be educated about their own heterosexuality as well as about homosexuality. The following are some of the salient learning points that we need to teach:

- *Accept our own sexuality.* In order for both pastors and lay people to minister effectively to gay and lesbian persons, we need first to accept our own sexuality. If there has been repression of our own sexuality, there may lie latent within us unresolved issues that can subconsciously hinder us from fully accepting who we are sexually. As the Christian Church comes to terms with its own inner attitudes and feelings toward sex, it will grow in health and usefulness by the hand of God in ministering to homosexual persons.

- *Learn the facts of the homosexual condition.* We need to provide books, articles, and resource materials on the latest findings of genetics and the social sciences as to the nature of homosexuality.

- *Listen to the stories of gay and lesbian persons.* We need to understand the real life experiences of one who discovers that his or her preferences are homosexual. Even better is getting to know homosexual persons in order to understand more deeply the complexities, mysteries, and agonies of the homosexual experience.

- *Distinguish between homosexual orientation and homosexual behavior.* Homosexually oriented persons equally display like all people something of the image of God, yet like all people are subject to a sinful nature and to certain particular temptations to sin.

- *Clarify the scriptural perspective on this subject.* We need to undertake a thorough study of the relevant biblical passages dealing with human sexuality and homosexual acts. The historic-biblical understanding of these passages should be brought to bear upon the recent well intentioned but untenable attempts at reinterpretation.

- *Minister to those struggling with homosexual desires and behavior.* The local church needs to be intentional about providing support for homosexual persons through Christian counsel, support groups, and fellowship groups.

We must not, however, only address the matter of homosexuality. We must give clear biblical teaching on heterosexual chastity outside of marriage and address the contemporary practice of living together before marriage. We must give clear biblical teaching and preaching on divorce and remarriage. Insofar as we fail to teach clearly on these sexual matters, our disapproval of same-sex unions will appear biased and arbitrary.

When I addressed the issue of homosexuality in the extended sermon series in the Fall of 2002, I found that a number of things happened. First, I found that delivering the messages created an atmosphere of openness in the church to talk about the subject. It gave people permission to talk about a matter that previously had been mentioned only in whispers. But beyond giving permission, we encouraged people to fully engage the subject. Many of our small groups suspended their normal study or fellowship agendas and followed up the messages by discussing them in their small groups. Discussion questions were provided to their leaders.

An atmosphere was created by the tone in which the messages were given. I strongly stressed that everyone of us in the church is battling something—envy, greed, lust, pride, loneliness, drug addiction, health problems, alcohol addiction, pornography addiction, gambling addiction, fear—some of us homosexuality. We are all in the same boat as the saying goes. And there is hope for us all! As their shepherd, I stressed my love for them. I stressed there was nothing that would keep me from loving them. We are all in this together so I challenged the church to help each other in their struggles. I challenged the church to roll up their sleeves and as brothers and sisters decide to be of whatever assistance and encouragement that God would have us be to one another. The discussions and interactions among the people which followed were indicative that they felt a new freedom to speak about homosexual issues in the open.

A second thing that took place was an openness on people's parts to share with me their struggles with homosexual thoughts and behavior. They perceived that I really did love them, cared for them, understood them at least to some degree and that I was there to help them in their struggles. When one of the teenage boys saw that homosexuality would be addressed in the series, he sat his parents down and shared with them his fears about being gay. His wise and loving parents listened as he spoke and affirmed their love for him in the midst of his questioning. After the first of the two messages the three of them came to talk to me. He shared again openly and honestly about his thought life, his feelings, and nagging questions. We talked about them. We talked about the normalcy of going through a period of time in our development where we each struggle with sexual identity. I encouraged them also to make contact with a local ministry staffed by persons who could share deeper insights from their own personal experiences of homosexuality. We prayed together and I assured the young man and his parents that I would be there for them.

Following the series, a woman confided to me that she had been involved in a ten-year lesbian relationship. It was a part of her life that she had kept even from her parents. But after listening to the messages, she felt she could talk openly to me and wanted me to know. She knew I was not going to condemn her or reject her. She felt confident enough that I would continue to love her. She really wanted to know what God wanted for her. That meeting was the first of several that we had together during which time we talked about her experiences and looked at Scripture passages. For some time she had attended a church that had taught that homosexual relationships were God-pleasing. She had learned new interpretations of the passages which said that they were irrelevant to loving, committed relationships today. We had rich and open exchanges in dialogue as we wrestled with what the Scripture is saying. I encouraged her also to contact a woman who had come out of the lifestyle. She followed up on the suggestion. She relayed to me how a chord was struck within her when the woman spoke of idolatry, of making the lesbian relationship more important than one's relationship with God. She is still on a journey, seeking God's will for herself, not presently in any relationship, and an active participant in the life of the church.

Without creating a safe atmosphere of openness, in all likelihood these persons would not have stepped forward for help. Others spoke to me about relating to relatives and friends who are gay or lesbian. We talked about the importance of accepting them as persons, of loving and caring, and of building relationships with them. I received numerous e-mails of appreciation and gratitude for addressing the issue from old and young alike. It was revealing that of all the sermons in the series, more cassette tapes were requested on homosexuality than any other subject. Our people are hungry to know what the Bible says about the issue and what is to be our attitude and practice towards friends and neighbors who are struggling with homosexual feelings and behavior.

Without addressing this subject in our churches, people who are struggling with homosexual tendencies will not know if we are understanding of their situation. Some believe their pastor will reject them if it becomes known. We can assure them that knowledge will not alter our love for them. Some live with the hidden fear that God hates them. We can assure them that God loves them and can and wants to forgive them and bring healing to them. Some live in the fear that if members of their congregation learn of their kind of sexual tendencies, they will want to exclude them from the Christian fellowship. We can assure them that their struggles will not exclude them any more than our own struggles will exclude us.

## A Community of Grace

The church is called by her Head to be a community of grace. We exist by the grace of God and we are to spread the grace of God to others. It is from within this community that the hope of the Gospel of Jesus Christ is to be brought to bear upon the needs and hurts of people. God in his grace and mercy has never left people without hope of healing. Immediately after the historic Fall, God promised that he would send the Messiah (Gen. 3:15), a promise that increased in clarity throughout the Old Testament. In the fullness of time Jesus, his Son, was born. When John the Baptist, suffering in prison for righteousness sake asked, "Are you the one who is to come, or are we looking for someone else?" Jesus replied, "Go back and report to John what you see and hear. The blind receive sight, the lame walk, and those who have leprosy are cured. The dead are raised and good news is preached to the poor." In other words, Jesus pointed to his own life lived out in real dusty history as the evidence that God is both good and powerful to redeem people from all the results of the Fall. The cross of Christ is our ultimate assurance of God's goodness and our hope of healing.

The fundamental Christian contribution to the one struggling with homosexual desires and behavior is not first in terms of law but in terms of grace. The gospel to one so struggling is not "Don't", but "God loves you and wants to help you". The Good News is that God so loved you that He gave his Son to be your Savior. One need no longer live under the umbrella of moral guilt. Sin has been overcome on the cross and forgiveness is freely extended as a gift. But not only forgiveness, from the cross flows also the hope of healing for the effects of the Fall.

However, not only did God send his Son, He also sent the Holy Spirit to make that salvation effective in terms of bringing about change in our human nature. He deeply desires to bring about change in us in the direction of conforming us more and more to the image of Christ. Because this is the direction of the change He desires to produce within us, the change is not always what we want or expect, but it is in accordance with his will which is always good and perfect. His will for us will always involve our dying daily to our own will that we may know the goodness of his gracious will. Our churches then need to be safe places for strugglers of all stripes to find grace and love and the power of release from the self-destructive grip of homosexual addictions and compulsions and anything else that has its hook in us. The church needs to be a safe place for strugglers of all types.

But a safe place is not what the average person in society thinks of when she thinks of the church today. Far from it. The average person perceives the church to be judgmental, intolerant, unloving, and filled with rather self-righteous hypocrites. We have the huge challenge then of communicating who we are to people in our society—including those struggling with homosexual feelings and desires. But who are we really? We are, as I told Ronald that evening, a massive multitude of moral foul-ups. We are not perfect people. We are sinners who don't have it all together in every area of our lives. We have bad habits. Some of us have a few screws loose. Others of us are a few eggs short of a full omelet. The elevator doesn't go all the way to the top for still others. We need to be honest with them as to who we are. But we also must tell them that we have been saved by God's grace and forgiven and that with the help of the Holy Spirit are encouraging one another as we walk arm in arm together in the direction of holiness of life.

We are a community of God's grace. We have been saved by his grace through faith. By his grace and with the help of His Spirit we are living in our baptismal grace, dying daily to sin in our lives and rising each day to newness of life. We are called to spread God's love and grace to others. That is who we are—and are to be.

## A Biblical Understanding of Love and Law

It is in talking about God's grace and love, however, that we must not become confused. For these words and concepts can be made to mean different things. Love can become something in and of itself severed from it moorings. It can be loosened from its reference point and become autonomous in its emphasis. This emphasis has been especially true in the Gay Christian Movement.

A centerpiece in the call today for homosexual relationships to be recognized and affirmed is the argument: "If a same-sex union is a loving, committed, monogamous relationship, it ought to be affirmed just like a heterosexual marriage." The quality (loving, caring) not kind (male—female) of relationship, it is argued, is what is important in God's eyes. God is a God of love. Love is the most important thing in the world. Therefore, love is the criterion by which every relationship is to be judged.

This is an argument that sounds so good and compassionate. Who after all can be against love? But it is an argument that reduces everything to love in a way that misconstrues both the Scriptures and the God of the Scriptures. Since this reductionism of love is currently so prevalent in both academia and popular culture, we need to look at it carefully and be clear concerning it.

The Gay Christian community and advocates of same-sex unions have brought two streams of thought together here. They have borrowed from Scripture the truth that love is the greatest thing in the world—which it is—and from the 'new morality' or 'situational ethics' of the 1960s the notion that love is an adequate criterion by which to judge every relationship—which it is not. The emphasis was already formulated in 1963 in the Friend's Report *Toward a Quaker View of Sex* which stated that "one should no more deplore 'homosexuality' than left-handedness" and "surely it is the nature and quality of a relationship that matters".[2] Since that time, a number of denominational sexual studies have built on this fundamental argument by saying in one way or another that permanent homosexual relationships characterized by love can be an appropriate and Christian way of expressing their sexuality. For Lutherans in the

Evangelical Lutheran Church in America of which I am a part, this direction was discernable in 1993 in a first draft of a social statement study document entitled "The Church and Human Sexuality: A Lutheran Perspective". A paper was presented at the task force's first meeting advocating that sexual relationships be evaluated on the basis of 'quality not kind'.[3]

What then is wrong with this argument? The biblical Christian cannot accept the basic premise on which this case rests, that is, that love is the only absolute, that beside it all moral law has been abolished, and that whatever seems to be compatible with love is in and of itself good, irrespective of all other considerations. This concept of autonomous love simply has no basis in Scripture or in the God of Scripture. Love is undoubtedly central to the Christian ethic. Nevertheless, without further guidelines, humans are notorious for drawing erroneous conclusions as to what love might entail in any given situation. We repeatedly find ourselves distorting genuine love in the name of 'love'. That is why in Scripture, love always needs law to guide it. Love has no internal moral compass of its own. Love is the motive. The Law is the moral compass that guides the motive in right action. In Scripture, love tells me *how* to do something. It does not tell me *what* to do. In stating the two great summary commandments, to love God and neighbor, Jesus did not do away with all the other commandments. On the contrary, Jesus said, *"If you love me you will keep my commandments"*, and Paul wrote *"love is the fulfilling of the law"*.

The Law was given to human beings not as a way to God. God rescued his people, the Hebrews, from their bondage in Egypt by delivering them through the Red Sea. It was purely his grace that rescued and saved them. They were saved not as a result of anything they had done. But then he led them to Mt. Sinai and gave them the 10 Commandments. Why? Because God wanted his children to remain free! He didn't want them to return to slavery. This is what the Commandments are for in the life of the Christian. The Christian has been rescued by God from bondage to sin through the waters of baptism. We are saved not as a result of anything we have done. It is God's grace alone that has rescued and saved us. But then Christ gives us the moral law that by living a life of obedience to that law, we might remain free and not return to slavery to sin. Disobedience to God's Law returns us to bondage and slavery, and eventual death. Obedience to His Law brings us freedom! No wonder Paul could say, *"I delight in the law of the Lord!"* It is the law of freedom! That is why within this community of grace called the church we share with people both the gospel and the law.

Love is not sufficient in and of itself, for God is not only Love but Holy. Of course, love is a very important quality in a relationship. But the quality of love can never authenticate a relationship. We think why this is the case. If love were the only test of authenticity, there would be nothing against polygamy, for a polygamist could certainly enjoy a loving relationship with several wives. An incestuous relationship might well qualify as a loving relationship. Following the logic of this position, there is no reason why there could not be a wide variety of life patterns: monogamy and multiple partnerships; partnerships for life and partnerships for a period of mutual growth; same-sex partners and opposite-sex partners; living in community and living in small family units. There would seem to be no limit to what could be justified in the name of love. If the love between two homosexuals justifies and makes normative and legitimate their homoerotic acts, then why would not the love between two people committing adultery justify the breaking of their marital vows?

This is not to deny that homosexual relationships can be loving. Indeed they can be and many are. But this love quality is not enough to justify them. The love of another must be according to the will of God. If it is contrary to the will of God, it is not love. True love is always compatible with God's law. True love is concerned for the good of the neighbor. And the highest human good is found in obedience to God's law and purpose, not in rebellion against them. The rhetorical question asked by Jerry Kirk, a pastor in the Presbyterian Church (U.S.A.) must be asked by all: "When God says such acts are sinful in His sight and contrary to His intentions, is it loving for us to tell such persons that their active sexual conduct is not sinful? Should we tell them that it is really okay, and even good?"[4] Quality of love is not an adequate yardstick by which to measure what is good or right. So while we are a community of love and grace, we understand that love and grace in its biblical sense.

In light of the biblical understanding that God is simultaneously Love and Holy, a God of wrath and a God of grace, how are we to understand God's relationship to homosexual persons? If we reflect on God's relationship to homosexual persons by analogy to human parents—particularly the response of parents to their homosexual children—we may gain greater clarity about God's regard for homosexual persons.

In his book, *Scripture & Homosexuality,* Marion Soards describes three basic ways parents react when sons and daughters inform them that they are gay or lesbian.[5] First, because the child is their own flesh and blood, after the initial shock some parents accept the news and become ardent defenders of their children's sexual behavior. (This is the same reaction that occurs with parents of heterosexuals who defend the premarital or extramarital activities of their children.) The reaction is all 'grace' with no judgment, and no reconciliation is needed. Second, on the opposite extreme, some parents immediately disavow their homosexual children because their sexual behavior is completely unacceptable to them. Again, parents of heterosexual children can have the same reaction when their children engage in sexual activities that are deemed inappropriate.) Here the reaction is all 'judgment' with no grace, and no reconciliation is possible. Third, there are parents who neither immediately reject nor accept their homosexual children. Rather, these parents struggle with the sexual activity of their sons and daughters. They cannot and do not approve of such sexual behavior. Yet their love for their children continues in spite of their children's sexual activity. (Once again, the parallel to parents of heterosexuals should be clear.) Here, at last, we find judgment, grace, and genuine yearning for reconciliation that informs and directs our own relationships to persons who are homosexuals.

With the evidence of Scripture before us—that God is love and that homosexual behavior is contrary to the will of God—I believe that God is like the loving human parents who in hearing the news of their children's homosexuality, nevertheless love their children with all their hearts while continuing to disapprove completely of their sexual activities. If God is like these parents, then we can make sense of the Bible's simultaneous images of God as both the God of wrath and the God of grace.

### Helping someone change

We turn our attention to those gay and lesbian persons in our congregations who now have been justified by God's grace and who have received Christ's forgiveness but who still have a strong homosexual orientation. What is to be their way of life? What is their calling?

These questions bring us face to face again with the very difficult question, "Can a homosexual change?" There are extremes of view on this matter. Even within the church you have some who maintain that asking a homosexual to change is like asking a leopard to change his spots. They can't do it. It is impossible. The orientation is too innate and fixed for there to be change. They come close to using deterministic language to describe the homosexual orientation. Therefore, it is argued, there are only two options for the homosexual person. Either, he has to accept the innateness of his condition, adjust, live with it and enjoy it, or not enjoy it but take a vow of celibacy and accept celibacy as a way of life.

There is great danger in defining homosexuality as unchangeable and fixed. The minute one does so, it almost precludes the possibility of change. The reality is that we don't really know how much change is possible for each individual. And when we come to look at how we can help people change, there is increasingly strong evidence that homosexuals can change, that homosexual orientation may not be as fixed as we once might have thought. What then do we do?

The first thing as we have suggested is to create an environment within our churches where change can take place. Our churches need to be warm, open, loving, caring and accepting places. Acceptance is the key. As human beings, we each have a deep need to be accepted by others. By loving and accepting people for who they are, we create an environment within which they can learn to see how God sees them and learn to accept themselves. Accepting others does not mean approving of all their behavior, but we are called to accept them in their struggles and failures as Christ has accepted us in ours.

Why is this acceptance so hard? The difficulty for us comes that in accepting others we at the same time have to accept the responsibility for working with the bad parts within ourselves. There are things inside of us that are working against the Word of God. Just think of something like drug or alcoholic or even promiscuity addiction. Think of the tremendous pain involved in dealing with it and facing up to it and the hurts that have flowed from it. It really is a painful thing to deal with and we must not underestimate the depth of the pain. But it is possible to change those things by facing them, accepting the situation and working at it. In the same way it is possible to change a large amount of homosexual orientation.

This change involves acceptance by others. For the homosexual it involves establishing wide friendships. People with homosexual orientations need an alternative family in which they are accepted for who they are. Many have been rejected and ostracized by their own families. They need a loving family in which they can feel loved. They need a caring family which can make up the deficiencies they experienced in their family of origin. Above all, they need to have normal non-erotic friendships with both males and females. In this way, a man can experience something that he yearned for but missed in the relationships in his own family. He can experience that sort of relationship where he gets approval from and some sort of identification with a man. This relationship will allow him in a sense to grow up emotionally wherein he can catch up to his body that has gone way ahead of him. Within the church fellowship, he needs to establish this sort of non-erotic friendship. It would be the same for lesbians.

In particular, small groups within a church fellowship can provide such an environment. Small groups are places where people can love and be loved, care and be cared for, know and be known, celebrate and be celebrated. It is where personal relationships can grow deep. It is where we can pray for one another, share our struggles and joys, and lovingly hold each other accountable. Small groups provide an environment within which the homosexual, on his long and difficult journey, can experience change.

In addition to the church fellowship and small groups, there is pastoral counseling by the church. Because of a pastor's demonstrated love and care for the flock, homosexual persons will seek us and be more open with us than with others. The pastor has the privilege of showing understanding and compassion to one who is struggling. The pastor has the privilege of sharing the gospel and giving guidance from God's Word. There are also specialized groups, many of them under the large umbrella of Exodus International, that minister specifically to those struggling with homosexual feelings and desires. These groups are usually staffed by persons who were once in the homosexual lifestyle and are no longer. There is great advantage for one currently struggling to talk with one who understands from personal experience the pain and hurts involved.

Then, if necessary, there is psychotherapy or professional counseling for those with deeper rooted problems. But psychotherapy in itself is limited if it is not surrounded by this loving and caring alternative family group which provides models of an alternate lifestyle and alternative relationships.

The church, then, ought to be a community within which change can take place. It is to be an environment within which repentant believers prone to certain sins are striving against their inner and outward expression. Hopefully, that is what the person with homosexual orientation within the church is doing. Hopefully, that is what we all are doing—struggling against sins, repenting daily, asking the Holy Spirit to make us more like Christ.

But what about the one who cannot change much? What about the one who is battling against his homosexual orientation but still finds it a strong and difficult tendency? What is such a one's calling? In light of the biblical teaching, I think we can only say that maybe this one has to view this as a call to celibacy. If one has called upon God's strength to help him change but there is little change, he may be called to trust God's grace to be sufficient to live the celibate life. The Christian's highest calling is that of *obedience* which is within the reach of all of us, rather than change, which is not easily or willfully attained and which varies from person to person.

By way of underscoring the possibility of change for the homosexual, there was a very interesting paper published some years ago in the *American Journal of Psychiatry* by two Christian psychiatrists, E. Mansell Pattison and Myrna Lloyd Pattison.[6] In the article the authors describe the change that occurred in 11 white, exclusively homosexual males. For all these men, before coming into contact with the church, the average rating on the Kinsey scale was six. That is the highest number on the Kinsey scale. The average age of the men was 23, with ages running between 17 and 35. They all had strong homosexual orientations since they were about age 11.

These men joined a Pentecostal church. The members of this church accepted them, loved them, and as a result they all became Christians. They were given loving acceptance in the context of small fellowship groups of prayer and Bible study. They were taught the Scriptures and were helped to repent and to forgive others and themselves, to deal with their pasts and to go on dealing from day to day with their homosexual orientation. Most of them came to find out that they were psychologically immature in relationships, which is something they hadn't realized before. They had thought they were quite normal. But within the context of the non-erotic relationships with men and women in the group, they were able to change.

At the time the article was written, seven of the eleven were happily married and had already been so for four years. The other four wanted to be married. On the Kinsey scale rating, five of them were now at zero. The other six varied on the scale between one and three. Not only did their overt behavior change, but their fantasy and dream life changed remarkably also.

## Calling People to trust God

Our central task as the church is to call people to trust God. What God is looking for when he speaks his Word of revelation to us is the response of trust. It is trust that accepts God's standards. The only alternative to heterosexual marriage is sexual abstinence. It is a hard standard. In our day it may even sound harsh and unreasonable. The secular world says, "Sexual fulfillment is a human right. It is essential to human fulfillment. To expect homosexual persons to abstain from sexual expression is to condemn them not only to frustration, but it can lead to neurosis and despair and even suicide. It is cruel and heartless and outrageous to ask someone to deny himself what is normal and natural for him." The Word of God, however, tells us something very different.

Despite the smooth illusions perpetrated by today's mass media, celibacy is not a fate worse than death and sexual gratification is not a sacred right. Sexual expression is not essential to human fulfillment. It is a good gift, but it is not given to all and it is not indispensable to humanness. Jesus Christ was single and fully human. Besides, God's commandments are good for us and not burdensome. In fact, obedience to his commandments brings freedom and rest. It is only those who resist his commands that become conflicted and enslaved.

At its bottom line, the whole discussion about homosexual practice is about trusting God. As Gagnon insightfully states: "[The whole sexuality debate] is about whether or not we have the right to define for ourselves what we can do on the basis of desires that we experience in life, or whether God has the right to transform us into the image of Jesus as God sees fit."[7] Does God love us and know what is best for us or do we know better than God? Whom shall we trust? The Christian response has always been, "God, even when everything within me says differently, I will nevertheless trust you".

The confidence the Christian can have is that with the Lord's call on our lives, we have the promise of his grace and strength to make choices that are pleasing to him. If God calls us to celibacy, abstinence is not only good but possible. To be sure it is made harder by the sexual obsession of contemporary society. It can be extremely painful. Homosexual lust that lurks in the depths is strong and powerful. But God's grace and strength is more powerful still. Indeed, all unmarried people experience the pain of struggle and loneliness. There is the constant voice of temptation. But whatever our 'thorn in the flesh' might be, God comes to us as he came to Paul and says, "My grace is sufficient for you, my strength is made perfect in weakness". We are called to trust this gospel of God's grace.

We live as a Christian community in the in-between time between the "already" and the "not yet". Already, through the indwelling Holy Spirit we experience the transforming grace of God. But not yet do we experience the fullness of redemption as we one day will. We live in a time of tension when the whole creation—including our bodies—groan in bondage and travail waiting, waiting for adoption and release. (Romans 8:23) We already have the first fruits of the Spirit, we have been set free from the power of sin through Christ's death, but we are still part of this fallen and disordered world and must struggle to live faithfully in the present. As we struggle we long for the not yet, the redemption of our bodies when we will experience release and complete transformation. In this time between the "already" and "not yet" some may find obedient abstinence the only faithful alternative to disordered sexuality.

The call to live celibate lives is countered with the argument that only a few have been given the gift of celibacy. Therefore, it would not be God's intention that those to whom he has not given this gift should be required to remain celibate. Sexual abstinence, it is argued, is only for those to whom the gift of celibacy has been given. But such is not the case. The gift of celibacy is the special supernatural ability to live fulfilled lives without the need for sexual fulfillment. Although celibacy is a special gift God has given to a few, God nevertheless calls all to sexual abstinence save within heterosexual marriage. God has given the spiritual gift of faith, the supernatural ability to just trust God in a way that is beyond the rest of us, to certain members of the Body of Christ, but he still calls all the rest of us to live by faith. God has given the spiritual gift of evangelism, the ability to speak the gospel to unbelievers in an effective way, to certain members of the Body, but still calls all of us to share the gospel in our own way and style. Just because he has given some the special gift of celibacy does not mean he does not call the rest of us to sexual abstinence outside of marriage.

God has created us. He knows us better than we know ourselves. He therefore knows what is best for us, what will bring us greatest fulfillment of our humanness. He knows that true human fulfillment comes only as we are conformed to the character of the One who created us. But our limited self-understanding and desires may lead us to search for human fulfillment in a very different direction. God has given human beings the gift of freedom. The glory and significance of being human is that we have been created to live not by instinct but by free choice. This freedom to choose is true of his sexual life whether he be heterosexual or homosexual. For each there is the freedom to choose to obey God's will for his sexuality. For each there is the freedom to choose 'not to'. Man is free to choose God's way or his own way. What he is not free to choose is the consequences of frustration, confusion, pain, and disorder that come from choosing against God's way. The choice before us in every area will always be, "Do I trust God's way to be best for me or will I try my own way"? The Christian's urgent call upon people's lives is to say 'no' to self and 'yes' to God.

# THIRTEEN
## Communities of Truth

Let us suppose that an environment for helping homosexual persons change has been created in our churches. Let us suppose members have repented of homophobia and ill treatment of homosexual persons and the church has become a loving, accepting, caring place, and yet there are persons within the church who are unrepentant. There has been loving admonition (I Cor. 4:14) and a loving call to repentance unto forgiveness. Jesus' instructions have been closely followed:

> "If your brother sins against you, go and tell him his fault, between you and him alone. If he listens to you, you have gained your brother. But if he does not listen, take one or two others along with you, that every word may be confirmed by the evidence of two or three witnesses. If he refuses to listen to them, tell it to the church . . . " (Matt. 18:15-17a)

What if all this has taken place but there is no evidence of a change of mind and heart or behavior? What if these unrepentant persons are following a steady and unresisting course of planned disobedience? Is there a limit to the doctrine of inclusiveness? In this Matthew passage, Jesus concludes: "and if he refuses to listen even to the church, let him be to you as a Gentile and a tax collector". (v. 17b) In the Epistle of John, John draws a distinction between those of us who sin and repent and get up and go on again (I John 1:6-10) and those who persist in their sin. (I John 2:4: 3:6-9) What is the church's responsibility in regard to these who are unrepentant?

## The Question of Church Discipline

The New Testament gives us teaching on discipline in the Christian fellowship. The Church at Corinth is an example of a church where there was sexual sin. The Corinthians were radical inclusivists and even prided themselves over a case of incest among them. In I Corinthians 5, there is the report of a young man acting irregularly in the sexual area. He was sleeping with his father's wife and was presumably impenitent and continuing in this relationship. It is instructive that we do not find Paul asking whether this man was having a loving, consensual relationship with his father's wife. There is no apparent inquiry as to whether it was a monogamous or committed relationship—which it might well have been. Paul apparently is not concerned about the quality of this relationship. He is concerned about the kind of relationship. Paul rebukes the Christian community for their tolerant, inclusive spirit. We find that the apostle demands that the man be disciplined by the church. The details of the discipline are not spelled out. We are told, however, the purpose of the discipline. The purpose of excluding this man from the church fellowship is that by being forced outside, he will wake up to the seriousness of his sin and turn in repentance to Christ for forgiveness and be restored to the church. The purpose of church discipline is for the salvation of the one disciplined.

Church discipline is necessary when one of its members specifically and persistently displays an attitude of rebellion with regard to any serious and unrepented sin. But note that in the case of homosexuality, it is not just someone with a homosexual orientation who occasionally slips up. Rather it is someone who says, "No, I am not going to choose God's way. I am going to go my own way and live the sort of life I want." There is this conscious and persistent attitude of rebellion against God's will.

Now within the Christian fellowship where there is a confessing of sins to one another and a confronting of one another in love, where there is an atmosphere of gentleness and prayer and caring, it should be very rarely necessary to exclude someone from the Christian fellowship. But very occasionally, it may be necessary. When it is necessary, it needs to be handled carefully and prayerfully, for the good of the one so disciplined, and to avoid needless pain and greater scandal. But when it becomes necessary, the purpose always must be for the sake of the restoration of the person. Church discipline within the Christian fellowship is part of the expression of both love and compassion for the individual disciplined and the judgment of God we are given the responsibility to exercise. It is a question of whether or not we love each other enough to hold each other accountable to God, and whether or not we love God enough to be faithful to his calling. But note carefully in the context of the homosexual question, it does not mean we exclude someone with homosexual or heterosexual or other sinful tendencies.

## Same-sex unions and ordination

The wider church is currently being asked by couples in committed love relationships to give its blessing to their unions as a homosexual counterpart to heterosexual marriage. The logic of the church doing so would be a recognition and affirmation of those homosexual unions as falling within the will of God. In taking this step, the church would be encouraging and strengthening such unions with its recognition, blessing and support.

Ought the church bless same-sex unions? No. From our conclusion regarding the sinfulness of homosexual behavior and from the normative nature of heterosexual 'one flesh' marriage, any affirmation of same-sex blessing or homosexual 'marriage' would not only be indefensible but would add to the rapid erosion of the term 'marriage' in our day. The church should continue to teach in the present what it has taught in the past that there are only two alternatives for God's human sexual creatures to live obedient lives of faithful discipleship: heterosexual marriage or sexual abstinence.

The wider church is also facing the decision of whether or not to ordain practicing homosexual persons. To clarify, this is not a question regarding the ordination of celibate, repentant, non-practicing homosexuals to positions of leadership in the church. It would follow from our clear distinction between homosexual *orientation* and homosexual *behavior* that no one sensing a true call from God to the ordained ministry should be excluded from ordination on the grounds of orientation alone. Those individuals who are particularly prone to temptations to engage in homosexual or extra-marital sexual activity should be encouraged and enabled to seek particular support and spiritual mentorship on their road to ordination. Wisdom would dictate that relationships of accountability be put in place. Once ordained, it would likewise be important to seek out the love and support of close Christian friends. Happy is the pastor who finds a small group of mature Christians within the congregation with whom to have the freedom to share the fact of his/her orientation and any problems associated with it. Such a group can also meet the need for non-erotic emotional relationships with people of both sexes.

Ought practicing homosexual persons be ordained? The answer again is no. Given the sinfulness of homosexual acts, it is clear that a homosexually oriented person who engages in such acts with another could no more be accepted into the ordained ministry than could a heterosexual person engaged in extra-marital sexual relationships.

An even more difficult matter is the reality of existing clergy in the church serving in positions of leadership who are avowed and practicing homosexuals. These ordained clergy do not believe that homosexual acts are intrinsically sinful. Here is a place where the reality of theological pluralism in the Church comes into full view in a practical way. Should the church honor this pluralism and allow avowed and practicing ordained homosexuals to serve in congregations that call them? Should the church allow some congregations to ordain active homosexuals, as their conscience leads them, and others of differing convictions to forbid ordination? Can homosexual behavior be treated as a minor matter of differing scruples of conscience within the church? Or must the church's decision-making body enforce a ban on ordination?

Paul gives us two contrasting principles on handling discipline in the church. On the one hand, there are certain matters dealing with scruples over holy days and diet. (Romans 14 and I Corinthians 8) Within the range of these issues, he urges the church to tolerate a diversity of opinion, warning against two abuses: judging another believer because of his or her scruples or liberty, and causing another believer to stumble by flaunting one's freedom of conscience. On the other hand, as we have seen with regard to incest in the church, Paul cannot treat this as a legitimate difference of conscientious conviction and demands that the church discipline the offender for his own sake and for the sake of the Gospel. ((I Corinthians 5 and II Corinthians 7) As our study has shown, the New Testament church did operate with a core of solid convictions about sexual morality which could not be made matters of opinion or debate. Where God's Word was clear on the intrinsic rightness or wrongness of sexual matters, the church called for obedience. Where God's Word did not speak an absolute word of right or wrong, there was room to follow the dictates of one's conscience.

Does the morality of homosexual behavior and the related question of the ordination of practicing homosexuals lie in the first area, that is, a matter of scruples of conscience? Or does it lie in the second area, that is, where God has spoken a clear word on the morality of homosexual behavior? Based on the findings of our study, it is clear that it lies in the second area.

The church's prophetic responsibility, both in issues of justice and morality, must be kept in mind here also. Ezekiel speaks powerfully of this responsibility:

"I have appointed you a watchman for the house of Israel; so you will hear a message from My mouth, and give them warning from Me. When I say to the wicked, 'O wicked man, you shall surely die,' and you do not speak to warn the wicked from his way, that wicked man shall die in his iniquity, but his blood I will require from your hand. But if you on your part warn a wicked man to turn from his way, and he not turn from his way, he will die in his iniquity; but you have delivered *your life.*"     Ezekiel 33:7-9

In light of these passages, it seems clear that the majority of leaders and lay people in the wider church who see homosexual behavior as sinful are justified in treating homosexual acts as a discipline issue in the church, rather than something that is to be tolerated or encouraged. In fact, their convictions *require* them to do so if they are to remain faithful to God, to his Church and to gay and lesbian people. To refuse to discipline would not only put themselves at spiritual risk but also the spiritual lives of homosexual persons and the rest of the members of the church.

On the basis of passages such as I Corinthians 5 and II Corinthians 7, I do not agree with those who maintain that the ordaining of practicing homosexual persons is merely a matter of conscience. But to those who remain unpersuaded that their practice is sinful, I would urgently point out that Romans 14 and I Corinthians 8 *requires* them to remain silent about it. They are required to remain silent out of respect for the consciences of the majority in the church who are (in their view) "weak in faith". Their self-affirming efforts to gain acceptance of ordination in the name of religious rights and honesty are in reality a violation of the law of love. Love requires that though they feel it permissible, they are not to openly indulge in a behavior which offends the consciences of most persons in the church and many in the world. Paul says that such a one puts a stumbling block before them (Romans 14:13; I Corinthians 8:9), injures them and causes their ruin (Romans 14:15), and destroys the work of God. (Romans 14:20; I Corinthians 8:11)

The conviction that the church should not ordain practicing homosexuals does not call for the church to commence a search-and-destroy mission against those pastors who are already in the pulpit or those leaders who are avowed and practicing homosexuals. Some cures are worse than the disease. Discipline needs to be done in all gentleness to avoid doing greater damage to the church. The church should make it clear that its desire is not for them to leave the church. They should be urged to remain. But the church should issue a general challenge to its practicing homosexual pastors and leaders to reconsider, to search their consciences and to move toward repentance. The church must then also, if necessary, take the further step to discipline those who insist on the public display of their behavior. If the attitude of a clergy person is one of persistently choosing that which is against the will of God, then out of love for them, here is one of those rare but necessary times when the church needs to discipline one of its own. The loving church is concerned about the salvation of all of its members and so disciplines. The unloving church does not.

## Staying the Course

What is a local church to do if the wider church of which it is a part decides for the moment to permit the ordination of active homosexuals? Are the leaders and members of churches to withdraw from that denomination? This agonizing decision is currently facing many local churches in mainline denominations. Although local situations may differ, both the Scriptures and Church history, it seems to me, give us precedents and directives in responding to these questions.

For denominations birthed out of the Protestant Reformation, the Reformation itself is a precedent. Despite the many errors and spiritual abuses and unbiblical teachings in the church of his day, Martin Luther never separated from the church. His burning desire was to reform the church from within, to direct the church back to the Scriptures. Luther was excommunicated and his teachings rejected by the church. He never selected the path of separation from the church. John Calvin also gave instructive words.

"As Augustine observes in disputing with the Donatists . . . private persons, if they see faults corrected with too little diligence by the council of elders, should not on that account immediately withdraw from the Church; and . . . . the pastors themselves, if they cannot succeed according to the wishes of *the hearts in reforming every thing that needs correction, should not, in consequence of this, desert the ministry.*"[1]

The freedom to proclaim and live out the gospel has not been curtailed in our denominations. We have the freedom to follow our consciences. There is widespread faulty thought and practice in the church today, to be sure. There are heretical teachings. But might not separation on account of these faults be only a form of Donatism, that is, a form of moral and intellectual arrogance which stems from spiritual pride? Is it not a failure of compassion for the church, when pastors and lay people separate themselves from a body at a time when that body desperately needs their support and witness to the gospel? The secular pressures in this modern time have terribly misshaped the minds and lives of many church leaders and members. There is much that is wrong. The Lord is undoubtedly weeping. But he is not abandoning his church as it goes through these rough waters, and we ought not to abandon the church either. The 8th Century missionary, Boniface said, "The church is like a great ship pounded by the waves of life's various stresses. Our job is not to abandon ship, but to keep it on its course."

The biblical witness is also strong in this direction. Despite the apostasy of the covenant people, God continued to send prophets to Judah and Israel. Elijah stood up strong against the false prophets of Baal and saw them ejected from leadership. When he became dejected by the counterattack of Jezebel, God reminded him that there were still 7000 in Israel that did not bend their knee to Baal. In the New Testament, Paul did not abandon the churches in Corinth or Galatia when they came under antichristian leaders. Rather, he chose to remain with the sheep and bark at the wolves. The New Testament antidote for dealing with spiritual dryness and false teaching was to *"contend earnestly for the faith"* with prayer, exhortation, and works of love. (Jude 3; 20-23) It was simply not Paul's mindset to separate from believers who are precious to the Father. Although Scripture does admonish, *"Do not be bound together with unbelievers; for what partnership have righteousness and lawlessness, or what fellowship has light with darkness"* (II Cor. 6:14), the application of this passage appears to be to Corinthian paganism, not to weak Christianity. In Ephesians 4:14-16, Paul exhorts believers to hold together, not separate from one another, so they not be carried about by every wind of doctrine, so that the body can grow healthy and strong. This antidote has proven itself worthy in history. Even though the church was riddled with the heretical doctrine of Arianism which claimed that Christ was less than God, the church father Athanasius remained steadfastly rooted in the church and in time saw the church return to soundness of doctrine. God's Truth is mighty and powerful and will prevail within the church, which the Holy Spirit has promised to lead into all the truth.

### An Urgent Apologetic Issue

On college campuses today, homosexuality is the single issue that Christians feel the most intimidated by and are most scorned for in holding their position. In many theological seminaries as well, homosexuality is the biggest issue under debate. Church denominations are split and torn by the debate. Apologetics is concerned with clarifying truth claims and giving reasons for holding to the central truths of the Christian faith. Homosexuality is an urgent apologetic issue today.

There is no question that in terms of public opinion the higher the prevalence of homosexuality, the more plausible it is for people to consider homosexuality as just another lifestyle as morally neutral as left-handedness. The media has clearly contributed to changing public opinion through its commitment to normalizing homosexuality. But in fact, the prevalence of homosexuality has no logical bearing on the moral debate or its moral status. The reason is that it is impossible to argue from an IS to an OUGHT. Even if 90% of the population were exclusively homosexual, that would prove nothing about whether it is right or morally neutral. If greed and pride are extremely common in our culture, does that make them morally neutral or morally right? In quite the other direction, Paul's reasoning in Romans 1 would argue that a high incidence of homosexual behavior can be understood as one evidence that a culture is in a state of significant distortion, confusion and rebellion

against God's created order. It is a culture that is a significant way down the road in terms of experiencing the effects
of having been given over by God to its own choice to reject
God in favor of human idols. A high incidence of homosexual activity, then, does not give moral justification to
anything, even though the media's use of statistics appears
to normalize it in the public eye.

The objection is raised that the bible's sex ethic is
unfair to homosexuals. God is charged with being cruel in
prohibiting homosexual acts to those whose orientation is
not of their own choosing. The Christian faith is unthinkable for many in that it allows for no morally legitimate way
to express homoerotic sexual identity. How do we respond
to these objections and charges?

If in fact God is cruel and unfair to homosexuals, then
it must be said that he is equally cruel and unfair to all of
us. Beginning with the fall into sin, every person has been
born with a predisposition or orientation to sin which is not
consciously or freely chosen. The Apostle Paul puts it very
strongly when he says we are born slaves to sin. (Rom. 6:17)
Heterosexuals and homosexuals alike are born with fallen
natures, a disposition to sin that we did not choose. God
allows us to be born in bondage to sin and yet holds us
morally accountable for our actions. It is a bondage from
which we cannot set ourselves free. That is why we need
Christ's redemption, that is, emancipation from slavery.
The heterosexual and homosexual are in precisely the same
place with regard to God's prohibiting immoral sexual acts
as those whose orientation is not of their own choosing.

Even after being redeemed, the Apostle Paul describes
the intense internal battle we continue to wage against sin.
He says in Romans 7:15: "For that which I am doing, I do
not understand; for I am not practicing what I would like to
do, but I am doing the very thing I hate." There is in the
Christian's life this ongoing battle with sin. It goes on
throughout the duration of the Christian's life for both
heterosexual and homosexual Christians. There is no basis
in Scripture for treating the process of growing in Christian
maturity for a homosexual Christian differently than for all
Christians, as if homosexual Christians are in a totally

unique category. All of us are fallen people, living in a fallen world and therefore predisposed to sin in different ways.

Is the Christian faith uncharitable because it does not allow for homoerotic expression? The argument is put forth that whereas heterosexuals who are single (unmarried, widowed, divorcees) are under the same admonitions as homosexuals to honor God with their bodies by remaining chaste, there is at least the hope and possibility of one day enjoying sex within legitimate marriage. But such a hope is not a possibility for the homosexual person. It needs to be acknowledged that this may be true for <u>some</u> homosexually orientated persons whose orientation runs deep within their being. But it must be pointed out that the unmarried woman who has strong sexual desires, whom no one asks to marry, is in the same place. She too is denied sexual expression. Both situations are a part of the abnormality of the fallen world. What is needed in both cases is compassionate understanding which moves the church to help the individual in every possible way.

In response to the charge that Christians are homophobic, there is no denying the fact that there are some Christians who are homophobic in the way that term is defined by the homophile movement. Some Christians do have neurotic fears and revulsions toward homosexuals. But the bible's prohibition against homosexual behavior is not homophobic. It does not separate out homosexual behavior for censure nor does it condone hatred toward any person. The bible considers all sexual activity that is not consensual and within the context of heterosexual, monogamous, faithful marriage to be immoral and falls short of God's norms. This teaching is particularly difficult in a sex-saturated culture like ours, not only for homosexuals but for heterosexuals as well. Our culture has made sexual freedom and experience an idol. We must be sexually active. Ironically, at the same time as we are looking to sex as the highest good in life, we are increasingly seeing the tragic and destructive fallout of making sexual freedom into an idol: unwanted pregnancies, abortions, single mothers, fatherless children, a whole array of sexually transmitted diseases, sexual addictions, the killer AIDS. In his book

*Straight and Narrow,* Thomas Schmidt meticulously documents the myriad of health problems connected to the gay lifestyle and the reason why male homosexual life expectancy, even without AIDS, is so much shorter than heterosexual male life expectancy.[2]

We pray and long for the day when freedom is redefined, or better properly defined, as freedom or self-control to exercise our sexuality within God's created purposes. This freedom is the kind of freedom discovered by pagans in the first century when they were converted to Christ. The new freedom that Christ gave them caused their lives to change most quickly and most dramatically in the area of sexual morality.[3] The pagans marveled at the Christians' sexual freedom! These Christians were free from being driven by their heterosexual and homosexual passions. The pagans marveled as they saw Christians free to live as chaste when single and monogamously when married.

The modern day Christian not only has the calling and responsibility to respond to objections against the Christian faith, he also has the calling and responsibility to live his life as a demonstration of the truth he professes. Nowhere is this more imperative for the current debate than in faithful marriage. One of the reasons that a strong gay rights movement has emerged is because heterosexual marriage has lost its beauty and moral authority, both of which are needed to make the normativity of marriage plausible and persuasive for people. Many gay men and lesbian women quite understandably point their fingers at the breakdown and ugliness of so much heterosexual marriage today. They quite reasonably point to the abuse of women and children which many have experienced firsthand in the so called traditional family. It is not surprising that many are commending or looking for alternative family forms. For heterosexual marriage to have any normative moral authority, it must be seen as functioning in a healthy way.

The challenge could not be greater for those who believe that faithful, caring, monogamous, heterosexual marriage is the Creator's norm and that it is good for individuals and families and society. It is incumbent upon

Christians today to be demonstrating before a watching world the beauty of marriage, something more than just living with prohibitions like not committing adultery. Our marriages and families have to positively demonstrate the goodness of God's sexual and family norms. The church needs to be a place where the love and care and nurture of husbands and wives for each other is encouraged and fostered, where children are raised in an atmosphere of emotional, psychological, spiritual and physical wholeness. Our homes need to be places where our children can grow up in healthy relationships with parents. Our marriages have to be attractive and life-affirming for men, women and children and reaching out beyond themselves to bless other people. Without that being a living reality, we cannot expect our verbal apologetics, either for the Christian faith or for the Christian sexual ethic, to be persuasive for anyone.

### A Community of Truth

The Church is to be full of grace. The Church, like its head, Christ, is also to be full of truth. We are called also to be a community that stands up for God's truth, not in an arrogant, pompous way, but in a kind and courageous manner. And the Church is called to speak that truth in love.

It is to be the case that the mind of Christ has so shaped our minds that we can lovingly but firmly say to practicing homosexuals that their behavior is contrary to the will of God, but that like with all other sins, Christ came to die for homosexual sin also. The mind of Christ is to so shape our minds that we can lovingly but firmly say to lesbian and gay activists that their idea of restructuring the family is just not a vision or plan that the follower of Christ can support. It will ultimately be destructive of persons, destructive of the family and lead toward the decay of society. We say this not because we are homophobic. We say this not because we are intolerant. And it is not because we are unloving or callous in spirit. We say this because we who are Christ's followers have learned to trust the wisdom of God. We have learned to recognize his Lordship over the ways we relate to one another in society as neighbors and spouses and parents and children. In Scripture, God's design for sexual expression is very clear and unambiguous. It tells us how marriages are to function and about family structure He has put in place. As Christian communities, we are called to be salt and light in society. As such we need to come out of the shadows and, for the sake of people and society, courageously declare God's intentions for sexuality and marriage.

There are some people who want to deny others their civil rights. I believe these people are wrong. We should not deny anyone in our society their basic civil rights. The church should, indeed, support civil rights for homosexuals. But sooner or later there is a line that gets crossed where the homosexual agenda begins to push on the rest of society in ways that are destructive of the common good. We have looked at Paul's words in Romans 1 where he speaks of the downturn of societies and cultures. I think God in our day is asking his Church to do something extremely difficult. He is a holy God and a loving God. As such He is calling his people to demonstrate both his love and his holiness simultaneously, not his love only and not his holiness only. Either one alone would be a caricature of God. I believe He is calling His Church today to at one and the same time build bridges and draw lines; to at one and the same time be communities of grace and communities of truth.

Having looked into the scriptures to see what they say about homosexual acts has confirmed my confidence that the church has been right over the ages in seeing homosexual behavior as intrinsically wrong. We now need God's grace to walk this tight rope of holding to this truth and speaking this truth in love. We are called to walk this line while under heavy fire of such slur words as homophobic and heterosexist. Under this barrage, it is all the more important that we love those who disagree with us. The Lord of the church calls us to love not only those who call us names, but to spend and be spent on behalf of those men and women who are suffering the sad and tragic consequences of living outside of God's created sexual boundaries which he has given us for our good.

Scripture is clear in our need as a church to reach out and open our doors and arms and hearts to people looking for help and hope. But at the same time, we are going to draw lines in the sand and warn those both inside and outside the church who would attempt to superimpose their social agenda on the biblical paradigm that we are going to stand up and stand firm and say, "No further! No further!" We do this for the simple reason that it is not God's way.

I believe this is the Church's calling in our day. And with God's help we can do it. In our local churches we can build bridges to help sexual strugglers who are reaching out for understanding and grace and release from the grip of their sexual confusion. At the same time we can draw definite lines in the sand and repeat the words of the great Reformer who said, "Here I stand. I cannot do otherwise. God help me."

# Endnotes

**Introduction**
1. Richard B. Hays, "Awaiting the Redemption of Our Bodies: The Witness of Scripture Concerning Homosexuality," in *Homosexuality in the Church,* ed. Jeffrey S. Siker (Louisville, Kentucky: Westminster John Know Press, 1994), 3-4.
2. Ibid. 4.

**Chapter One: Four Common Myths**
1. Virginia Ramey Mollenkott. "Overcoming Heterosexism—To Benefit Everyone" in *Homosexuality in the Church: Both Sides of the Debate* ed. Jeffrey S. Siker (Louisville, Kentucky: Westminster John Knox Press, 1994). 148.
2. Stanton L. Jones & Mark A. Yarhouse. *Homosexuality: The Use of Scientific Research in the Church's Moral Debate* (Downers Grove: InterVarsity Press, 2000), 33.
3. F. Earle Fox & David W. Virtue. *Homosexuality: Good & Right in the Eyes of God?* (Alexandria, Virginia: Emmaus Ministries, 2003), 251.
4. Ibid.
5. Ibid.
6. Jones & Yarhouse, 36.
7. Ibid. 36-7.
8. Jeffrey Satinover. *Homosexuality and the Politics of Truth* (Grand Rapids: Baker Books, 1996), 53-4.
9. Jones & Yarhouse, 46.
10. Richard Cohen, M.A. *Coming Out Straight: Understanding and Healing Homosexuality* (Winchester, Virginia: Oakhill Press, 2000), 21.
11. Daniel L. Olson. "Talking about Sexual Orientation" in *Faithful Conversation: Christian Perspectives on Homosexuality* ed. James M. Childs Jr. (Minneapolis: Fortress Press, 2003). 115.
12. A. Dean Byrd. "The Innate-Immutable Argument Finds No Basis in Science." http://www.narth.com/menus/born.html.
13. Ibid.
14. Ibid.
15. John White. *Eros Defined* quoted in *The Church and Homosexuality,* Michael Green, David Holloway, David Watson (London: Hodder And Stroughton, 1980) 49.
16. Stanton L. Jones and Don E. Workman. "Homosexuality: The Behavioral Sciences and the Church" in *Homosexuality in the Church: Both Sides of the*

*Debate* ed. Jeffrey S. Siker (Louisville, Kentucky: Westminster John Knox Press, 1994). 97.

17. Gary Glenn. "Texas Case Spotlights 'Gay-on-Gay' Violence," Internet article, October 2003.

18. Jones & Yarhouse. *Homosexuality: The Use of Scientific Research in the Church's Moral Debate*, 54.

19. Michael Green, David Holloway, David Watson. *The Church and Homosexuality* (London: Hodder and Stoughton, 1980), 66.

20. Jones and Workman. "Homosexuality: The Behavioral Sciences and the Church", 103.

21. Ibid.

22. Byrd. "The Innate-Immutable Argument Finds No Basis in Science."

23. Minnesota Christian Chronicle. "Study finds homosexuals can change orientation if they try." May 17, 2001. See www.mcchronicle.com

24. Ibid.

25. Byrd. "The Innate-Immutable Argument Finds No Basis in Science."

## Chapter Two: Causes of Homosexuality

1. Daniel L. Olson. "Talking about Sexual Orientation" in *Faithful Conversation: Christian Perspectives on Homosexuality* ed. James M. Childs Jr. (Minneapolis: Fortress Press, 2003). 113.

2. Stanton L. Jones and Don E. Workman. "Homosexuality: The Behavioral Sciences and the Church" in *Homosexuality in the Church: Both Sides of the Debate* ed. Jeffrey S. Siker (Louisville, Kentucky: Westminster John Knox Press, 1994). 103.

3. "Homosexual Urban Legends: The Series 'Born Gay'. http:/ www.traditionalvalues.org/urban/three. php.

4. Ibid.

5. Jones and Workman. 101.

6. "Homosexual Urban Legends: The Series 'Born Gay'."

7. Ibid.

8. Ibid.

9. Merton P. Strommen. "Homosexuality: A Youth Issue" in *Christian    Sexuality: Normative & Pastoral Principles* ed. Russell E. Saltzman (Minneapolis: Kirk House Publishers, 2003) 95.

10. Jeffrey Satinover, M.D. *Homosexuality and the Politics of Truth* (Grand Rapids, Michigan: Baker Books, 1996). 77.

11. Merton P. Strommen. Ibid.

## Chapter Three: The Gay Lifestyle & Agenda

1. Video documentary *The Gay Agenda: The Report* by Ty & Jeannette Beeson. 1993.

2. Stanley, Monteith, MD. *The Gay Agenda: The Report*

3. A. Dean Byrd. "Governor Dean Misunderstands Origins Of Homosexual Behavior." http://www.narth.com/docs/dean.html.

4. Marshal K. Kirk and Erastes Pill. "The Overhauling of Straight America," *Guide,* November, 1987.

5. *The Independent.* Thursday 16 October 2003.

6. Alan Sears and Craig Osten. *The Homosexual Agenda: Exposing the Principal Threat to Religious Freedom Today* (Nashville: Broadman and Holman Publishers, 2003) 16-27.

7. Ibid. 23.

8. Marshal Kirk and Hunter Madsen. *After the Ball: How America Will Conquer Its Fear and Hatred of Gays in the 90s* (New York: The Penguin Group, 1989) 381.

9. Kirk and Madsen. 382-383.

**Chapter Four: Four Christian Views**

1. H. Kimball Jones, *Towards a Christian Understanding of the Homosexual* (New York: Associated Press, 1966), 108.

2. Robin Scroggs, *The New Testament and Homosexuality: Contextual Background for Contemporary Debate* (Philadelphia: Fortress Press, 1983), 127-129.

3. Walter Wink, "Homosexuality and the Bible," in *Homosexuality and Christian Faith: Questions of Conscience for the Churches,* ed. Walter Wink (Minneapolis: Fortress Press, 1999), 46-47.

**Chapter Five: The Great Divide—Biblical Authority**

1. George Muedeking, "Christ's Scripture or Scripture's Christ: Is It an Either-Or?" http://www.churchmoraldebate.com/theold/christscript.htm

**Chapter Six: Interpreting the Bible**

1. Martin Luther, quoted in *The Church & Homosexuality,* Green, Michael, Holloway, David, Watson, David. (London: Hodder and Stoughton. 1980.) 69.

2. I am indebted for much of the material in this section to Barry Seagren, "Hermeneutics" L'Abri Fellowship Lecture. No. BS-8

3. Thomas Aquinas, quoted on p. 56 of Bishop Michael Doe, *Seeking the Truth in Love: The Church and Homosexuality* (London: Darton, Longman and Todd Ltd, 2000)

**Chapter Seven: The Heterosexual Norm**

1. Robert A.J.Gagnon, *The Bible and Homosexual Practice: Texts and Hermeneutics* (Nashville: Abingdon Press, 2001), 187.

2. Michael Green, David Holloway, David Watson, *The Church and Homosexuality* (London: Hodder and Stougton, 1980), 74

3. Ibid. 94.

4. Ibid. 74.

5. Gagnon, 189-190.

**Chapter Eight: Old Testament Biblical Fences Around Marriage**

1. John Boswell, *Christianity, Social Tolerance, and Homosexuality: Gay People in Western Europe from the Beginning of the Christian Era to the Fourteenth Century* (Chicago: The University of Chicago Press, 1980), 93-94.

2. D. J. Atkinson, *Homosexuals in the Christian Fellowship* (Oxford: Latimer House, 1979), 81.

3. J. N. D. Kelly, *The Epistles of Peter and Jude* (A. & C. Black, 1969), 258.

4. Derek Kidner, *Genesis* (Tyndale Press, 1967), 137.

5. Derrick Sherwin Bailey, *Homosexuality and the Western Christian Tradition* (London: Longmans, Green and Co., 1955), 23.

6. D. J. Atkinson, 98-99.

7. Derrick Sherwin Bailey, *Homosexuality and the Western Christian Tradition* (London: Longmans, Green and Co., 1955), 55.

8. Letha Scanzoni and Virginia Ramey Mollenkott. *Is The Homosexual My Neighbor?* (San Francisco: Harper & Row Publishers, 1978), 60-61.

9. John Boswell, *Christianity, Social Tolerance, and Homosexuality: Gay People in Western Europe from the Beginning of the Christian Era to the Fourteenth Century* (Chicago: The University of Chicago Press, 1980), 101-102.

10. Ibid., 104.

11. Richard Winter. "Homosexuality." Chesterton, Indiana: L'Abri Cassettes. Catalogue No. S232.

12. Robert A .J. Gagnon, *The Bible and Homosexual Practice Texts and Hermeneutics* (Nashville: Abingdon Pres, 2001), 121.

13. Boswell, *Christianity, Social Tolerance, and Homosexuality,* 100.

14. Gordon J. Wenham, *The Book of Leviticus* (Grand Rapids, Michigan: William B. Eerdmans Publishing Company, 1979), 279.

## Chapter Nine: New Testament Biblical Fences Around Marriage

1. John Boswell, *Christianity, Social Tolerance, and Homosexuality: Gay People in Western Europe from the Beginning of the Christian Era to the Fourteenth Century* (Chicago: The University of Chicago Press, 1980), 109.

2. Ibid., 110.

3. Ibid., 110-111.

4. Ibid., 112.

5. Robin Scroggs, *The New Testament and Homosexuality* (Philadelphia: Fortress Press, 1983), 117.

6. Ibid., 116.

7. Ibid., 122.

8. Richard B. Hays, "The Biblical Witness Concerning Homosexuality," in *Staying the Course,* rd. Maxie Dunnam and H. Newton Malony (Nashville: Abingdon Press, 2003), 71.

9. Ibid., 197.

10. Richard B. Hayes, "Hays Challenges Boswell's Interpretation of Biblical Position on Homosexuality," in *The Religion & Society Report,* 1996. 4-5.

11. Richard Winter. "Homosexuality." Chesterton, Indiana: L'Abri Cassettes. Catalogue No. S232

12. Derrick Sherwin Bailey, *Homosexuality and the Western Christian Tradition* (London: Longmans, Green and Co., 1955), 38.

13. Richard Winter.

14. Richard Lovelace, *Homosexuality and the Church* (London: Lamp, 1978), 94.

15. Scroggs, 115.

16. Ibid., 122.

17. Ibid., 114-115.

18. Hays. "Hays Challenges Boswell's Interpretation of Biblical Position on Homosexuality."

19. Scroggs, 46.

20. Ibid., 47-48.

21. Hays. "Hays Challenges Boswell's Interpretation of Biblical Position on Homosexuality."

22. Robin Scroggs, *The New Testament and Homosexuality: Contextual Background for Contemporary Debate* (Philadelphia: Fortress Press, 1983), 106-108.

23. D. J. Atkinson, *Homosexuals in the Christian Fellowship* (Oxford: Latimer House, 1979), 91.

24. John Boswell, *Christianity, Social Tolerance, and Homosexuality: Gay People in Western Europe from the Beginning of the Christian Era to the Fourteenth Century* (Chicago: The University of Chicago Press, 1980), 107.

25. Ibid.

26. Martti Nissinen, *Homoeroticism in the Biblical World: A Historical Perspective* (Minneapolis: Fortress Press, 1998), 118.

27. Scroggs, *The New Testament and Homosexuality,* 120-121.

## Chapter Ten: Analogy Arguments

1. Gagnon, Robert A.J. AThe Bible and Homosexual Practice: Theology, Analogies and Genes" p. 5. A Study for Congregations. Paper handout.

2. Meilaender, Gilbert. First Things "What Sex Is—And Is For." April 2000. Number 102. p. 45-46.

3. Gagnon.

4. Forde, Gerhard. "Law and Sexual Behavior," footnote 13

## Chapter Eleven: Attitudes and Understanding

1. Richard F. Lovelace. *Homosexuality: What Should Christians Do About It?* (Old Tappan: Fleming H. Revell Company, 1978), 129.

2. Mardi Keyes. "Challenge of Homosexuality: Speak Truth In Love," (Chesterton, Indiana: L'Abri Cassettes), Catalogue No. 2923.

## Chapter Twelve: Communities of Grace

1. Olson, Daniel L. "Talking about Sexual Orientation: Experience, Science, and the Mission of the Church" in Faithful Conversations: Christian Perspectives on Homosexuality. 110.

2. Stott, John. Quoted in *Issues Facing Christians Today* (Southampton: Marshall Morgan & Scott, 1984) 314.

3. Klein, Leonard R. "Lutherans in Sexual Commotion," in *First Things.* May 1994. Number 43. p. 34.

4. Kirk, Jerry. Quoted in *Welcoming But Not Affirming: An Evangelical Response to Homosexuality* by Stanley Grenz (Louisville: Westminster John Knox, 1998) 8-9.

5. Soards, Marion L. *Scripture & Homosexuality.* (Louisville: Westminster John Knox Press, 1995), 66-67.

6. E. Pattison and M. Pattison, "Ex-Gays: Religiously Mediated Change in Homosexuals," American Journal of Psychiatry. 137. (1980). 1553-62.

7. Gagnon, Robert A. J. "The Bible and Homosexual Practice: Theology, Analogies, and Genes" originally appeared in the Nov/Dec 2001 issue of *Theology Matters.* 2.

## Chapter Thirteen: Communities of Truth

1. Richard F. Lovelace. *Homosexuality: What Should Christians Do About It?* (Old Tappan: Fleming H. Revell Company, 1978), 122.

2. Thomas E. Schmidt. *Straight and Narrow?* (Downers Grove: InterVarsity Press, 1995) 112-130.

3. Mardi Keyes. "Challenge of Homosexuality: Speak Truth In Love," (Chesterton, Indiana: L'Abri Cassettes), Catalogue No. 2923.

# Selected Bibliography

Atkinson, D. J. 1979. *Homosexuals in the Christian Fellowship.* Oxford: Latimer House.

Bailey, Derrick Sherwin. 1955. *Homosexuality and the Western Christian Tradition.* London: Longmans, Green and Co.

Boswell, John. 1980. *Christianity, Social Tolerance, and Homosexuality.* Chicago: The University of Chicago Press.

Bradshaw, Timothy, ed. 1997. *The Way Forward? Christian Voices on Homosexuality and the Church.* London: Hodder & Stoughton.

Childs, James M. Jr., ed. 2003. *Faithful Conversations: Christian Perspectives on Homosexuality.* Minneapolis: Fortress Press.

Cohen, Richard. 2000. *Coming Out Straight: Understanding and Healing Homosexuality._* Winchester, Virginia: Oakhill Press.

Dallas, Joe. 1991. *Desires in Conflict.* Eugene, Oregon: Harvest House Publishers.

Dallas, Joe. 1996. *A Strong Delusion.* Eugene, Oregon: Harvest House Publishers.

Doe, Bishop Michael. 2000. *Seeking the Truth in Love: The Church and Homosexuality._* London: Darton, Longman and Todd Ltd.

Dunnam, Maxie D., and Malony, H. Newton. ed. *Staying the Course.* Nashville: Abingdon Press.

Field, David. 1979. *The Homosexual Way—A Christian Option?* Downers Grove: InterVarsity Press.

Forde, Gerhard O. 1995. "Law and Sexual Behavior." *Lutheran Quarterly.* Spring Issue. Vol. 9.

Fox, F. Earle and Virtue, David W. 2003. *Homosexuality: Good and Right in the Eyes of God?* Alexandria, Virginia: Emmaus Press.

Gagnon, Robert A.J. 2001. *The Bible and Homosexual Practice Texts and Hermeneutics.* Nashville: Abingdon Press.

Gagnon, Robert A.J. AThe Bible and Homosexual Practice: Theology, Analogies, and Genes.

Gagnon, Robert A.J. and Via, Dan O. 2003. *Homosexuality and the Bible: Two Views* Minneapolis: Fortress Press.

Gill, Sean, ed. 1998. *The Lesbian and Gay Christian Movement: Campaigning for Justice, Truth and Love.* London: Cassell.

Goddard, Andrew. 2001. *God, Gentiles and Gay Christians: Acts 15 and Change in the Church.* Cambridge: Grove Books Limited.

Gomes, Peter J. 1996. *The Good Book: Reading the Bible with Mind and Heart.* New York: William Morrow and Company, Inc.

Green, Michael, Holloway, David, Watson, David. 1980. *The Church and Homosexuality.* London: Hodder and Stoughton.

Grenz, Stanley J. 1998. *Welcoming But Not Affirming: An Evangelical Response to Homosexuality.* Louisville: Westminster John Knox.

Jones, H. Kimball. 1967. *Toward a Christian Understanding of the Homosexual.* London: SCM Press Ltd.

Jones, James H. 1997. *Alfred C. Kinsey: A Public / Private Life.* New York: W.W. Norton & Company.

Jones, Stanton L., and Yarhouse, Mark A. 2000. *Homosexuality: The Use of Scientific Research in the Church's Moral Debate.* Downers Grove: InterVarsity Press.

Kirk, Marshall, and Madsen, Hunter. 1989. *After the Ball: How America Will Conquer its Fear and Hatred of Gays in the 90's.* New York: Penguin Books.

Koester, Craig R. 1993. AThe Bible and Sexual Boundaries". *Lutheran Quarterly* 7:375-90.

Leal, Dave. 1996. *Debating Homosexuality.* Cambridge: Grove Books Limited.

Lovelace, Richard F. 1978. *Homosexuality: What Should Christians Do About It?* Old Tappan: Fleming H. Revell Company.

McNeill, John J. 1977. *The Church and the Homosexual.* London: Darton, Longman and Todd Ltd.

Moberly, Elizabeth R. 1983. *Homosexuality: A New Christian Ethic.* Cambridge: James Clark.

Nissinen, Martti. 1998. *Homoeroticism in the Biblical World: A Historical Perspective.* Minneapolis: Fortress Press.

Perry, Troy D. with Swicegood, Thomas L.P. 1990. *Don't Be Afraid Anymore: The Story of Reverend Troy Perry and the Metropolitan Community Churches.* New York: St. Martin Press.

Pittenger, Norman. 1976. *Time for Consent: A Christian's Approach to Homosexuality.* London: SCM Press Ltd.

Ramsey, Paul. 1965. *One Flesh: A Christian View of Sex Within, Outside and Before Marriage.* Bramcote Notts: Grove Books.

Reisman, Judith A. 1998. *Kinsey: Crimes & Consequences.* Arlington, Virginia: The Institute for Media Education, Inc.

Reisman, Judith A. and Eichel, Edward W. 1990. *Kinsey, Sex and Fraud: The Indoctrination of a People.* A Lochinvar-Huntington House Publication.

Saltzman, Russell E. ed. 2003. *Christian Sexuality: Normative & Pastoral Principles.* Minneapolis: Kirk Publishing House.

Satinover, Jeffrey. 1996. *Homosexuality and the Politics of Truth.* Grand Rapids: Baker Books.

Scanzoni, Letha and Mollenkott, Virginia Ramey. 1978. *Is The Homosexual My Neighbor?* San Francisco: Harper & Row Publishers.

Schmidt, Thomas E. 1005. *Straight & Narrow? Compassion & Clarity in the Homosexuality Debate.* Downers Grove, Illinois: InterVarsity Press.

Sims, Bennett J. 1977. *Sex and Homosexuality: A Pastoral Statement.* Atlanta: Communications Department Episcopal Diocese of Atlanta.

Scroggs, Robin. 1983. *The New Testament and Homosexuality.* Philadelphia: Fortress Press.

Sears, Alan, and Osten, Craig. 2003. *The Homosexual Agenda: Exposing the Principal Threat to Religious Freedom Today.* Nashville: Broadman & Holman.

Siker, Jeffrey S. ed. 1994. *Homosexuality in the Church: Both Sides of the Debate.* Louisville: Westminster John Knox.

Soards, Marion L. 1995. *Scripture and Homosexuality.* Louisville: Westminster John Knox.

Stott, John. 1984. *Issues Facing Christians Today.* Southampton: Marshall Morgan & Scott.

Stott, John. 1998. *Same-Sex Partnerships? A Christian Perspective.* Grand Rapids: Fleming H. Revell.

Strommen, Merton P. 2001. *The Church & Homosexuality: Searching for a Middle Ground.* Minneapolis: Kirk House Publishers

Vasey, Michael. 1995. *Strangers and Friends: A new exploration of homosexuality and the Bible.* London: Hodder & Stoughton.

Von Rad, Gerhard. 1956. *Genesis.* London: SCM Press LTD.

Bradshaw, Timothy. ed. 1977. *The Way Forward: Christian Voices on Homosexuality and the Church.* London: Hodder & Stoughton.

Wenham, Gordon J. 1979. *The Book of Leviticus.* Grand Rapids: William B. Eerdmans Publishing Company.

Williams, Don. 1978. *The Bond That Breaks: Will Homosexuality Split The Church?* Los Angeles: BIM, Inc.

Wink, Walter, ed. 1999. *Homosexuality and Christian Faith: Questions of Conscience for the Churches.* Minneapolis. Fortress Press.